D1269119

Mexican Patterns

MEXICAN PATTERNS

A DESIGN SOURCE BOOK

Chloë Sayer

PORTLAND HOUSE
NEW YORK

This edition published by Portland House
distributed by Outlet Book Co Inc.
a Random House Company
225 Park Avenue South
New York, New York 10003

Copyright © 1990 Studio Editions

The right of Chloë Sayer to be identified as author of this
work has been asserted by her in accordance with the
Copyright, Designs and Patents Act, 1988.

All rights reserved. No part of this publication
may be reproduced, stored in a retrieval system,
or transmitted in any form or by any means, electronic,
mechanical, photocopying, recording or otherwise,
without the prior permission of the copyright holder.

ISBN 0–517–01491–2

Printed and bound in Malaysia

h g f e d c b a

Introduction

Contemporary Mexican textiles have a vigour unsurpassed elsewhere in Latin America. It is more than four and a half centuries since the Spanish Conquest, yet nearly sixty Indian peoples still live in Mexico. Many wear distinctively patterned costumes, which vary from region to region and even from village to village. These may be achieved with textile techniques inherited from the ancient civilizations of the Mixtec, the Aztec or the Maya. Traditionalism of this kind has become rare in most areas of the world, where indigenous clothing is increasingly kept for parades and festive occasions. European and North American visitors to rural Mexico are invariably impressed, therefore, when they see Indian families wearing elaborately woven or embroidered clothing in their everyday lives.

Since the Conquest in 1521, a large number of textile designs have been modified or wholly inspired by the outside world, but the pre-Conquest legacy is still apparent in many Indian communities. As the archaeologist George C. Vaillant has noted, design and the arrangement of elements are more important than form in Indian art. Unfortunately for the study of Mexican textiles, few early cloth samples have survived. Excesses of heat and damp, in conjunction with acid or alkaline soils, have contributed in most regions to their decay. Despite these hazards, however, a few vestiges have been recovered from dry caves, which often served as burial sites, and from the sacred well at Chichén Itzá, used by the ancient Maya for sacrifice and for making offerings to the gods. Carbonized textile fragments, encased and preserved over centuries by thick mud, have been brought up from the depths.

Codices, clay figurines, stone carvings, mural paintings and polychrome pottery vessels offer further insight into pre-Conquest styles of dress and decoration. Although many of these representations are highly stylized, some are remarkably naturalistic. Carved stone lintels from the Maya site of Yaxchilán suggest not only the garments worn, but even the patterning of fabric. Pottery spindle whorls and stamps also provide invaluable information about pre-Hispanic design. They show abstract motifs, calendrical elements, deities, animals both real and mythological, reptiles, birds, flowers and foliage. Before the Conquest pottery stamps may have been used to embellish cloth.

The writings of the Spanish *conquistadores* contain many references to textiles. Although quick to condemn the 'savage' and 'pagan' customs of their new subjects, they nevertheless admired the artistry displayed by spinners, dyers and weavers. In a report to the King of Spain, Hernán Cortés wrote: 'Moctezuma gave me a large quantity of his own textiles which, considering they were cotton and not silk, were such that there could not be fashioned or woven anything similar in the whole world for the variety and naturalness of the colours and for the handiwork.'

The Codex Mendoza, commissioned in 1541–2 by the first Mexican viceroy, includes a pictorial record of tribute paid to the Aztec by subjugated peoples within their empire. As an important element, textiles were frequently portrayed with the required designs. Tributary mantles were decorated in a profusion of styles. According to Diego Durán, the Spanish friar, 'some of them had rich fringes done in colours and feather work; others had insignia on them, others serpent heads, others jaguar heads, others the image of the sun, and yet others had skulls, or blowguns, figures of the gods — all of them embroidered in many coloured threads and enriched with the down of ducks, all beautifully and curiously worked.' Clearly the élite dressed with great splendour in pre-Conquest Mexico, yet displays of wealth were governed by rigorous discipline. Status in Aztec society required the use of specific garments, adornments and design motifs. As believers in predestination, the ancient Mexicans were accustomed to searching for signs and symbols, and to vesting all things, even a jewel or a colour, with an inner meaning.

The abolition of the old social hierarchy and the imposition of Christianity under Spanish rule had far-reaching effects on native dress. Friars and governors, determined to eradicate cultural traits which they saw as 'uncivilized', outlawed many forms of personal adornment such as face and body painting. Meanwhile new materials, textile techniques, clothing styles and design motifs were introduced into Mexico. Spain's impressive and varied heritage was shared in part with her European neighbours, but it also owed much to nearly eight centuries of occupation by the Moors, who brought with them skills and aesthetic principles acquired in Asia Minor and Egypt. In Mexico the scope of these outside influences was further enlarged after 1565, when the Philippines came under Spanish domination. Great galleons from the Orient, packed with fine cloth, porcelain, lacquerware and other imports gave added impetus to Mexican craftwork (see Plates 7, 8). Today Mexican textiles derive their richness and vitality from the fusion over centuries of these different traditions.

Although modern Mexicans are predominantly *mestizo* (of mixed European and Indian descent), the Indian population is estimated at around eleven million, which is roughly 15 per cent of the national total. Mexico's widely varying geography has contributed greatly to the sense of independence felt by many indigenous peoples. In remote areas some communities still lead a surprisingly marginal existence; others, in more accessible regions, have joined the national culture, but retain many ancient customs and beliefs. Although a few Indian peoples continue to worship a pantheon of gods whom they identify with the forces of nature, most are nominally Catholic.

Continuity with the past is reflected in the material culture of many groups. Natural surroundings still provide the raw materials for house-building, basketry, potting and other ancient crafts. Textile skills centre chiefly on the creation of clothing. In Western culture it is easy to take textiles for granted and to consider their manufacture as removed from daily life. In Mexico, however, women work hard to clothe themselves and their families. Costume acts as a bond which unites people from the same community, proclaiming their geographical and cultural origins.

In some regions women's clothing has changed very little in hundreds of years. Wrap-around skirts and waist-sashes are often worn with *huipiles*, or tunics, made from vertically joined cloth webs. Another ancient garment is the *quechquemitl*, or closed shoulder-cape, which is traditionally assembled from two rectangles or squares. Today the *quechquemitl* is combined with the blouse — Spain's most significant contribution to female dress. The *rebozo,* or rectangular shawl, favoured in Indian and *mestizo* communities, evolved during the Colonial period. Women in some villages also use head-cloths and carrying-cloths.

Since the Conquest male dress has undergone more changes than female dress. Spanish friars were shocked by nudity, and men came under pressure to adopt shirts and to abandon loincloths in favour of trousers; these are often worn with woven waist-sashes. To make up for the lack of pockets in Indian dress, men usually carry their belongings in shoulder-bags. During cold weather Indians and *mestizos* sometimes wear a woollen *sarape,* or blanket, with an opening for the head. Like the *rebozo,* this garment evolved under Spanish rule. In addition to the male and female garments just described, many Indian households use home-produced blankets and all-purpose cloths, or *servilletas.*

As in pre-Hispanic times, clothing is assembled without tailoring from rectangles or squares of material. The elegance and beauty of Indian garments depend less on construction than on the texture, colour distribution and surface decoration of cloth. Weavers work as they did before the Conquest with white cotton and, in some areas, with a tawny-brown strain known as *coyuche.* Sheep's wool and Asiatic silk, introduced during the Colonial period, are also used in Indian Mexico. Often yarn is spun in traditional fashion with the aid of a spindle. Synthetic colourants have become increasingly popular, but natural dyes from vegetable animal and mineral sources are still preferred in a few villages (see Plate 98). Rich blue-black tones are created with indigo; red is obtained with brazilwood and logwood, or with ground cochineal insects, while on the Pacific coast cotton is occasionally dyed purple with the secretion of shellfish (see Plates 79, 80).

Although archaeological remains confirm the existence of *ikat* techniques in northern Peru, no pre-Conquest examples have so far been found in Mexico. If not indigenous, this technique may have been introduced under Spanish rule, either from south-east Asia or from the Middle East via Italy and Mallorca. *Ikat-*dyed yarns are patterned before they are woven: stretched between two sticks, they are tightly bound at predetermined intervals with thread. When the skein is dipped in the dye bath, covered portions are 'reserved'. During the eighteenth and nineteenth centuries *rebozos*, or rectangular shawls, were frequently woven with *ikat*-dyed warp threads. Sometimes embroidered motifs were bordered by *ikat*-produced triangles or stepped chevrons, but often the entire *rebozo* was delicately patterned with reptilian markings, characteristically blurred where the dye has penetrated the bindings. Nationally *ikat* remains the most admired form of decoration for shawls. Using imported Chinese silk, artificial silk or cotton, weavers in Santa María del Río and in the Toluca Valley produce delicately dappled cloth in two or more colours (see Plates 13, 14). Patterning may be dense or sparse, according to cost, and makers have names such as *lluvia* (rain) and *llovizna* (drizzle) to describe different styles.

The availability of commercially produced yarns, which come ready-dyed, has influenced design in most areas of Mexico. Acrylics and other synthetic fibres are fast replacing wool, silk and cotton. Although industrial colours rarely match the subtle tones obtained with natural methods, many weavers welcome the saving in time and effort. Garments carry ever larger areas of patterning, and bright colours are enthusiastically combined. The Huichol Indians, who live among the mountain ranges of the western Sierra Madre, now favour acrylic yarns in luminescent shades of lime green, acid yellow and shocking pink (see Plates 59–60). For fine work these may be re-spun in traditional fashion.

Textile patterning is achieved in a multiplicity of ways. Apparently simple garments such as the *huipil* or the *quechquemitl* can display a wealth of designs. As in pre-Hispanic times, these are often achieved on the backstrap, or stick, loom. While one end is attached to a tree or post, the other is attached by a strap to the weaver herself, who controls the tension of the tightly stretched warps with her body. Although long webs of cloth are sometimes woven, the width is limited by the weaver's armspan. Deceptively 'primitive' in appearance, with no rigid framework, this type of loom nevertheless lends itself to a wide range of effects which it would be hard to imitate commercially. In parts of northern

Mexico there exists a second type of Indian loom: square or rectangular in shape, it consists of a rigid frame built close to the ground. Weaving with native looms remains an almost exclusively female pursuit, but the Spanish treadle loom is worked by men. Introduced soon after the Conquest, it is ideally suited to the production of blankets, skirts and long lengths of cloth.

During weaving, designs are created in the cloth. Plain weaving allows the formation of warp and weft stripes (Plates 75, 85b); checks are made by mixing warp stripes with weft bands. With tapestry weaving, weft threads of different colours are used; these do not travel the width of the loom, but move across selected areas, building up patterns in the cloth. The *sarape* represents the perfect match on Mexican soil of two foreign elements — wool and the treadle loom. Tapestry-weavers in some centres work with dyed and undyed yarn to create a range of geometric patterning (see Plate 15), yet none can rival the complexity of eighteenth- and nineteenth-century examples (see Plates 1–5).

During the Colonial period production centres grew up in several areas, but the most famous was Saltillo in the northern state of Coahuila. By manipulating richly coloured weft threads *sarape*-weavers achieved dazzling effects, which led Náhuatl-speaking Indians to talk of *acocemalotíc-tilmatli*, or 'rainbow mantles'. Gradually the term 'Saltillo' was applied to similarly patterned *sarapes* from other towns. Characteristic designs included small triangles, rhomboids, hour-glasses and ovals grouped round a central lozenge or medallion. Patterning may have evolved from a number of sources, including native ones. Archaeological textile remains from Chihuahua display diamond motifs, but imported textiles from the Philippines, China, the East Indies, Holland and Spain may also have been influential. According to some estimates, the weaving of a Saltillo *sarape* of the classic period could have required up to 500 hours. Although the *sarape* lost none of its splendour in the nineteenth century, purists consider that increasing opulence marked a decline in quality. Gold and silver metallic threads, silk and newly invented aniline dyes were used in the creation of *sarapes* for the rich, who regarded them as prized possessions.

10

Double weaving requires great skill. Achieved with two sets of warps, it is a speciality with backstrap weavers in just a few communities. Among the Huichol, the Cora and the Otomí, bags and sashes are plain-woven in two layers: motifs are identical on both sides of the cloth, but the colours are reversed, so that a red bird on a blue background becomes a blue bird on a red background (see Plates 23, 58–62). Gauze weaving, used to create open-meshed cloth, has a wide distribution. With this largely manual technique selected warps are crossed, then secured by the weft. In villages such as Atla and Xolotla Nahua weavers elaborate all-white cotton *quechquemitl* of figured gauze. Motifs include human figures, animals and double-headed eagles (see Plate 52b). With warp patterning, raised designs are formed in the cloth. Warp threads, manipulated by hand, are periodically moved over and under varying numbers of weft threads. Sashes are embellished in this way in a number of regions including Chihuahua, where Tarahumara women create geometric patterning on rigid log-looms with undyed wool (see Plate 70).

The versatility of native looms is further demonstrated by weft-brocading. Used in conjunction with plain and gauze weaves for almost all categories of clothing, this popular construction relies on supplementary weft threads which form superstructural designs. Some weavers specialize in working in white on a white background, but most employ brightly coloured threads (see Plates 91a, 92, 99, 100). This type of work is often mistaken by the uninitiated for embroidery. Warp-brocading, used in San Simón de la Laguna and other villages, employs supplementary warp threads for the patterning of sashes (see Plates 25, 26, 33, 37). Closely related to weft-brocading is weft-loop weaving. With this technique supplementary weft threads are pulled up with a pick to form raised designs.

Although most weavers carry their designs in their heads, relying on memory and the imagination, cloth fragments from worn-out garments usefully serve as *muestras*, or samplers, for occasional consultation. Often illiterate and without formal education, many weavers reveal a remarkable and intuitive grasp of mathematics as they divide and subdivide warp threads to form different groups of motifs. Asked to explain her rapid calculations, Ana Cecilia Cruz Alberto — an Otomí weaver from San Miguel Ameyalco, who created the magnificent brocade-patterned textile in Plate 27 — replied, 'But it is my fingers, not my head, that do the counting. They think for me.'

The structure of cloth makes it inevitable that woven designs should be characterized by a certain angularity. Embroidery can offer greater freedom; it also allows women to personalize bought cloth. Since the nineteenth century, sales of commercially produced cotton cloth have escalated in Indian Mexico. In villages where cloth is still home-woven, however, it may be elaborately patterned with embroidery; some women even combine decorative stitching with woven designs. It is difficult, given the scarcity and the fragmentary nature of pre-Conquest textiles, to say which stitches were current before the introduction of Spanish embroidery methods and the arrival of imported textiles from China and the Philippines. Today garments such as blouses display increasingly large areas of needlework. Fine embroidery is achieved with cotton, silk, artificial silk, wool and, increasingly, acrylic yarns.

In many communities designs are perpetuated by samplers, which serve not only as teaching aids but also as reminders in adult life. Few, if any, samplers have endured from the early period of Colonial rule, but the Victoria and Albert Museum in London owns several later examples, embroidered between the end of the eighteenth century and the start of the twentieth (see Plate 9). Many of the stitches and design motifs shown are still current. Several very elegant eighteenth-century *rebozos* have also survived. Motifs, colourfully and minutely satin-stitched with silk thread, included rural and city scenes, bullfights, processions and the coats of arms of wearers. The magnificent example shown in Plates 7 and 8 features costumed figures, fountains and other Mexico City landmarks of the period. It has been suggested that needlework of this type may have been inspired by the long embroidered silk scarves worn by female courtiers in Imperial China.

Today satin-stitching remains extremely popular: animals, birds, flowers and foliage embellish a variety of *servilletas* and garments. Blouse panels embroidered in San Juan Chilateca and

San Antonino Ocotlán resemble miniaturized flower gardens (see Plate 73). By contrast, gala clothing on the Isthmus of Oaxaca displays vast and colourful flowers; worked with a special embroidery hook, these flamboyant designs may originally have been inspired by imported Oriental shawls (Plate 74a). Satin-stitching is also used with great imagination by Otomí villagers in Tenango de Doria, Santa Monica and San Pablito. Small cloths and large wall-hangings, aimed at the tourist market, conjure up a rainbow-coloured world of fairy-tale creatures and plants, suggested as much by fantasy as by observation of nature (Plates 20–22). This trend shows that demand can, on occasion, stimulate inventiveness. In most regions where textiles are regularly sold to outsiders, however, standards drop and the quality of work suffers.

Running stitch, identified in pre-Conquest cloth samples, is also put to decorative use by many women. This form of embroidery is popular in Nahua villages throughout the Puebla highlands, where the neck and sleeve panels of blouses display bird, animal and plant motifs (see Plates 42, 43, 46). Sometimes, as in Atla, patterning is negative — it is the white cloth which conveys the design (see Plate 45). Looped stitches such as chain are employed, and frequently combined with different stitches, in several villages (see Plate 78). Few embroidery techniques can rival the popularity of crossed stitches, however. Cross stitch, long-armed cross stitch and herringbone have had enormous impact in Mexico; in some areas they are even taking over from flat stitches. Huichol women, who are highly skilled in the art of needlework, pattern ever larger areas of clothing by this method (see Plates 64–69).

In some communities women draw their designs on to the cloth, although in others this practice is frowned upon. With most styles of embroidery, threads are carefully counted; often the resulting designs are as stylized as those achieved through weaving. In recent years women have come increasingly to rely on *cuadrillé*. This type of open-meshed commercial cloth is ideally suited to cross stitch, although finished work is usually less fine than formerly. Another innovation has been the sewing machine. Blouses frequently combine hand-embroidery with machine-stitched areas of whirlpool patterning (see Plate 43a). Early photographs show that by 1898 Zapotec women on the Isthmus had already begun to decorate everyday *huipiles* with narrow machine-embroidered bands. Today wide bands featuring superimposed lines of chain stitch run parallel with the sides and hem; if well done, this work has the delicacy of filigree (see Plate 74b). Existing patterns are known by such names as 'jaguar', 'star' or 'crab-vendor', and new ones are constantly evolving.

Many additional textile methods are used for the creation of designs. Drawn threadwork requires individual threads to be drawn out from the cloth; the rest are then regrouped, bound to produce a square-meshed ground, and reinforced with decorative stitching. Birds, monkeys, human figures, crosses and sacred hearts pattern the nineteenth-century altar cloth shown in Plate 10. Beadwork also achieved great popularity during the last century; sadly, rising prices are pushing this form of decoration beyond the reach of many people. In villages such as San Pablito, however, small glass beads are sewn down individually on to the panels of blouses and shirts; shimmering and brilliantly coloured designs include horses, birds and squirrels (see Plate 17). Alternatively, glass beads may be netted: during Huichol festivals men display hat-bands, sashes, shoulder-bags, bracelets and necklaces, patterned in a profusion of ways (see Plate 63). Satin ribbons have many uses; often they are appliquéd to cloth to conceal seams, or hemmed in points to embellish neck openings (see Plates 81a, 87b).

The long evolution of Indian costume, and the many outside influences that it has sustained, make it difficult to ascertain the origins of most design motifs. In recent decades there has been a vogue for copying geometric elements from archaeological sites such as Mitla, although resulting textiles are generally intended for sale to outsiders. There seems little doubt, however, that some of the designs which pattern indigenous clothing are genuine survivals from earlier times.

In her book *Design Motifs on Mexican Indian Textiles*, Irmgard Weitlaner Johnson has identified a wide range of pre-Hispanic geometric forms. These include chevrons, triangles, zig-zag lines, hooks, spirals, spots, squares, rectangles, parallelograms, di-

14

amonds, X-shapes, crosses, S- and Z-patterns and stepped frets. In contemporary Mexico these may be woven or embroidered, used singly, repeated over a wide expanse of cloth or intricately combined.

Waist-sashes display a variety of designs. Outer edges are often adorned with zig-zag borders (see Plates 35a, 70). Zig-zag effects are popular, too, with the Huichol for woven and embroidered clothing, and with the Amuzgo for the decoration of *huipiles* (see Plates 83, 84). Spots add interest to the over-all design of many textiles. Sometimes they pattern the bodies of animals portrayed on Otomí double-woven bags (see Plate 23); squares are similarly used as filler elements by embroiderers in San Pablito (see Plates 16, 18). Rectangles occur where web joins have been decoratively over-stitched (see Plate 87a). Some Aztec *huipiles* portrayed in the codices feature a single horizontal rectangle below the neck; this custom persists in the Chinantec village of San Lucas Ojitlán, where a small section of ribbon is sewn on to the cloth (see Plate 86). X-forms, combined with other motifs, appear in Plates 58 and 85a. Although the Latin cross is of post-Conquest origin, crosses with arms of equal length are indigenous to Mexico; they too serve as filler elements in San Pablito (see Plate 18).

The triangle offers textile workers wide scope. It appears on Tarahumara sashes and Mixtec *huipiles* from San Pedro Jicayán (see Plates 70, 80). Two inverted triangles give an hour-glass form. Alternatively, two or four triangles can create diamonds and squares (see Plate 66a). Adjoining triangles provide serrated borders. Parallelograms are no less versatile; eight-point stars or flowers, formed from eight parallelograms, are current among the Otomí, the Nahua, the Huastec and the Huichol (see Plates 19, 48, 55b, 65). Diamonds are perhaps the most widely used geometric design. Concentric and aggregate diamonds once dominated the centre of *sarapes* from Saltillo and other towns (see Plates 1–5). Diamonds remain a key factor in the Chiapas highlands, where richly brocaded *huipiles* and sashes from modern Maya communities such as Magdalenas and San Andrés Larrainzar echo the patterning of stone lintels from Yaxchilán. In this region diamonds are often bordered by hooks — a device similarly

15

favoured by the Huichol (see Plates 69, 98a, 100). Concentric diamonds with a serrated outer edge also feature on textiles from various places (see Plate 28).

Angular and curvilinear spirals pattern many garments. In the Nahua village of Atla and in various Chinantec communities these are embroidered (see Plates 51b, 85a, 87a). According to José Luis Franco, the *ilhuitl*, or double-spiral motif, was a pre-Hispanic solar symbol which denoted a day of festival. Today S- and Z-shaped spirals occur in many forms and regions. Otomí and Nahua *quechquemitl* in San Pablito and Santa Catarina exhibit positive and negative angular spirals (see Plates 19, 48), while blouses from San Pablito and other villages display simpler, curvilinear variations (see Plates 16, 47). Among the Huichol interlocking and single spirals also pattern embroidered garments and woven bags (see Plates 58, 65, 66b).

Xicalcoliuhqui, or stepped-fret patterning, also has a long history in Mexico. Found extensively in pre-Hispanic codices, buildings and clothing, it was thought by the late Miguel Covarrubias to represent the stylized head of the Sky-Serpent and to symbolize the god Quetzalcóatl. This is just one of several theories, however. José Luis Franco, by contrast, sees it simply as a decorative element conveying the notion of duality central to pre-Hispanic thought. Today garments in several communities carry borders consisting of angular stepped frets (see Plate 68).

Nature inspires many design motifs. Although some appear recent in origin, others recall pre-Hispanic styles. Zoomorphic patterning on woven Mazahua sashes from San Simón de la Laguna are traditional in feeling (see Plates 35b, 37b). Birds are a popular subject with most Indian groups. The Huave, who live near salt-water lagoons on the coast of Oaxaca, adorn their brocaded *servilletas* with a profusion of aquatic birds such as pelicans and seagulls. Diminutive humming birds on bags and sashes from Santo Tomás Jalieza delicately take nectar from flowers, while large birds with elaborate plumage pattern embroidered *huipiles* in Chinantec and Mazatec communities (see Plates 72, 86, 87b, 88–90).

Animals provide a still wider range of decorative elements. Represented in this book are embroidered squirrels, rabbits, and an armadillo (see Plates 43a, 88, 22). Monkeys, fish, serpents, dogs and other indigenous creatures also appear on numerous garments. The deer is perhaps the animal most often shown. As with other zoomorphic designs, portrayals range from the highly stylized to the naturalistic; here the deer is rendered through embroidery, warp patterning, double weaving and even figured gauze (Plates 30b, 42, 51a, 52b, 60a). With the Conquest a new range of animals entered the field of Mexican textiles. Today horses are represented on *sarapes* and other articles of clothing; with their plumed tails they prance across *huipiles* in San Miguel Metlatonoc, and blouses in San Pablito and Cuetzalan (see Plates 16, 46b, 82). Occasionally goats also feature on bags and blouses (see Plates 23a, 43b). Lions topped with crowns or flowers occur in textiles from the Huasteca and other regions (see Plates 50a, 56a). No Indian garment, however, carries as many zoomorphic elements as Mixtec shirts and trousers from Santa María Zacatepec. Embroidered areas resemble colourful menageries replete with minuscule birds, cats, foxes, scorpions and other creatures. Crocodiles, iguanas, butterflies and even centipedes may also be shown in different parts of Oaxaca.

Although human figures are usually combined with other motifs, in San Juan Colorado they sometimes people all-purpose cloths, or *servilletas* (see Plate 77). In Santo Tomás Jalieza handsome warp-patterned sashes display *danzantes*, or dancers with plumed headdresses from the Zapotec Feather Dance (see Plate 71). Flowers and foliage abound in most regions. Stylized vine motifs pattern woven garments in Amuzgo villages such as Xochistlahuaca (see Plates 83, 84); in other villages ancient and recent motifs are embroidered on blouses, skirts, *huipiles, quechquemitl* and men's kerchiefs (see Plates 31a, 41, 57). Frequently flowers are shown with eight petals (see Plates 28, 58). Vases or pots of flowers, often surrounded by birds, are a recurrent theme (see Plates 38a, 49, 56a). In their most developed form such designs are described as 'trees of life'. As noted by Irmgard Weitlaner Johnson, some variations may be due to European influence, although sacred trees were linked in the past with the four cardinal directions.

A similar debate centres on the origin of the double-headed

17

eagle. This immensely popular design is found throughout Indian Mexico, yet many people assume that it stemmed from the crowned Habsburg eagle of Colonial times (see Plate 11). In the pre-Hispanic era double-headed birds appeared on pottery, spindle whorls and seals. It seems reasonable, therefore, to look on contemporary representations as survivals. Although the examples included in this book are too numerous to list fully, Otomí, Nahua, Huastec, Huichol and Mixtec forms are represented (see Plates 18, 29, 52b, 55b, 65, 78, 80). In a few rare instances double-headed deer and four-headed birds are also depicted.

Extreme stylization makes many apparently indigenous designs virtually indecipherable to outsiders. Shown in Plate 52a is a weft-brocaded sash from the mountains of Zongolica in Veracruz. Designs portray combs, breads, pathways and various species of plant. Their meaning is obvious to local women, but unreadable to anyone else. Another extreme case of stylization is recorded by Irmgard Weitlaner Johnson: among the Amuzgo of Xochistlahuaca, the butterfly is represented by a single triangle. This is, in her words, 'the ultimate in abstract representation'. Indian terms used to describe many designs are equally obscure; when translated into Spanish, their meaning may be even less clear. Trique weavers in San Andrés Chicahuaxtla define different styles of patterning as 'sube y baja' (goes up and down) or 'rapido' (rapid) (see Plate 92).

By contrast a number of designs are unequivocally post Conquest. The Agnus Dei adorned numerous all-white altar cloths during the last century; today Latin crosses are displayed on men's shirts in the Tzotzil village of Huistán. Christianity also inspires the patterning of textiles with churches in San Miguel Ameyalco, while blouses in Coacuila portray Virgins surrounded by pink cherubs (see Plates 27, 44). Wit and imagination characterize the embroidered wall-hanging shown in Plate 21: dancing devils and winged angels, satin-stitched in bright colours, circle the sun in pairs. Lettering is often used to decorative effect. Near Lake Pátzcuaro, Purépecha weavers embellish warp-patterned sashes with names, dates and popular refrains. In the Puebla highlands embroidered blouse yokes sometimes feature words or single letters positioned at random (see Plates 41, 44). The national emblem is a favourite theme. To commemorate the founding of the Aztec city of Tenochtítlan, Mexico adopted an ancient symbol: an eagle perched on a prickly pear with a serpent in its beak. Today this design is found on embroidered cloths, Otomí double-woven bags and Nahua skirts from Acatlán (see Plates 20, 23b, 53).

Just as factory threads affect the colouring of textiles, so printed pattern sheets and booklets influence design in many areas. Cross-stitched horsemen, mules, parrots, peacocks and heavily shaded, Western-style roses have replaced more traditional motifs on several garments. Calendars and advertisements may also be absorbed into the Indian design vocabulary. During the late 1940s an unusual example of outside inspiration was reported by Bodil Christensen. A blouse yoke from the Nahua region of Huauchinango depicted a man with a large fish on his back; this motif had been suggested by the current label on bottles of Scott's Emulsion. Today the range of non-indigenous designs is greatest among the Zapotec of Teotitlán del Valle, Oaxaca. Formerly tapestry-patterned *sarapes* were characterized by a large central flower, or star. Now treadle-loom weavers reproduce the paintings of Braque, Miró and Escher for the tourist trade, or imitate Navajo designs for North American retailers.

Indigenous costume has never been static. Decoration is often subject to local fashion trends, and innovations may be quickly copied by fellow villagers. During the 1980s Mazahua *quechquemitl* in villages such as San Francisco Tepeolulco received increased decoration (see Plates 31b, 32). A similar vogue among Otomí girls in Santa Ana Hueytlalpan is responsible for lavishly patterned blouses with densely embroidered yokes, silver braid and sequins.

In regions where change has been extensive, design motifs have largely lost the significance of earlier times. In the Chiapas highlands, however, patterns continue to carry various levels of meaning. Research undertaken during the 1970s and 80s by Walter F. Morris and Martha Turok provides an analysis of weaving symbols in Magdalenas and other modern Maya communities. The fusion of indigenous and Christian beliefs is represented by the often complex patterning of garments. Used in different combinations, designs perpetuate traditional agricultural and astronomical concepts. Diamonds, for example, are flat representations of the earth, which is thought to be cube-shaped; their corners correspond to the four cardinal points, and also to the four corners of the sky and the maize field. Plant elements such as beans, maize and flowers are accompanied by highly stylized zoomorphic motifs. These include spider monkeys, bats and bees, and carry names like *Santo* ('Saint') and *Gran Santo* ('Great Saint'). Such symbols are almost certainly related to pre-Conquest deities, although today they serve as intermediaries between villagers and the Catholic hierarchy. As in the past, colours are identified with the cardinal directions.

The Huichol also express their beliefs through costume. Isolated by the high mountain ranges of the western Sierra Madre, members of this marginal group continue to worship a pantheon of deities associated with the forces of nature. Dress is looked on as an expression of faith. According to one legend, 'a fine Huichol man's costume is what first enabled the Sun Father to rise in the sky and shine'. Waist-sashes, which are identified with serpents because of their long, winding shape and because of the reptilian markings which they often display, serve as requests for rain and for the benefits which rain brings — namely good crops, health and a long life. Designs on clothing protect wearers from harm and serve as visual prayers. Zig-zag lines that suggest lightning are associated with rain, while the white *totó* flower that grows during the wet, maize-producing season is both a petition for and a symbol of maize. Magical powers are attributed to birds, as it is thought that they can see and hear everything during their flight above the earth, and different birds are associated with different deities. The eagle belongs to Grandfather Fire. Thought to guard the young maize, it may be shown with a single head, or from the front with two heads to represent both profiles (see Plate 65).

In Indian Mexico it is impossible to separate the secular and the sacred. In the Chiapas highlands and in many other regions the saints are dressed in diminutive indigenous garments, patterned in the style of the village. Many ancient rituals are associated with the arts of weaving and embroidery. Textiles in Mexico may still be part of everyday life, but they also retain a spiritual and a ceremonial importance rarely found in the world today.

Acknowledgements

Plates 1, 2, 3, 6: Michael Caden; Plates 7a, 7b, 8: courtesy of Mrs P.A. Tritton (photographs D.W. Gardiner); Plates 4, 5, 9, 10, 11, 12: Victoria and Albert Museum, London; Plates 13–100: David Lavender.

The following Indian groups are represented in the plates:

Otomí	Plates 16–30a
Mazahua	30b–37, 38b
Nahua	38a, 39–55a
Huastec	55b, 56a
Tepehua	56b
Totonac	57
Huichol	58–69
Tarahumara	70
Zapotec	71–74
Mixe	75
Mixtec	76–82
Amuzgo	83–84
Chinantec	85–87
Mazatec	88–90; 91b
Huave	91a
Trique	92
Maya (Tzotzil and Tzeltal)	93–100

The Plates

PLATE 1

Classic Saltillo **sarape**, *treadle-woven during the last half of the eighteenth century. It is characteristically patterned with small lozenges and other geometric elements; these are grouped round a serrated concentric diamond centre. Woollen weft yarns are natural, or dyed with cochineal and vegetable colourants such as indigo and brazilwood. 92" × 51" (233.6 × 129.5 cm). Collection Michael Caden.*

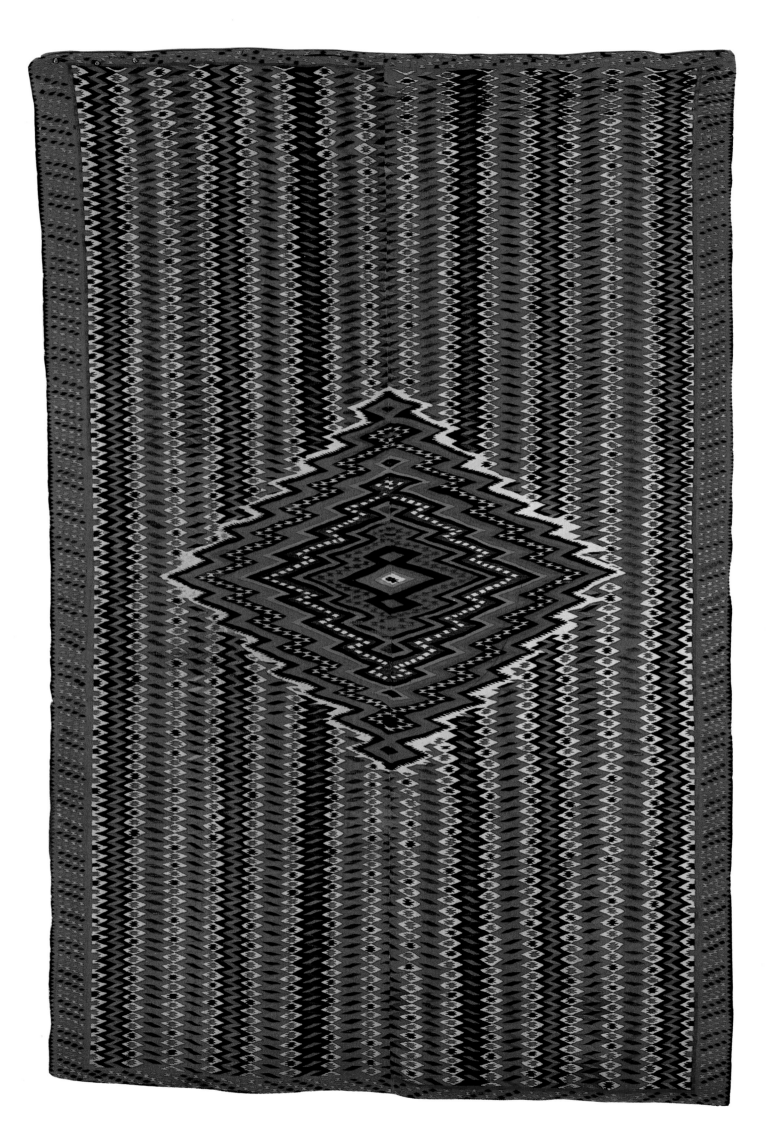

PLATE 2

Classic Saltillo sarape, *treadle-woven during the last half of the eighteenth century, with spot repeat patterning. Woollen weft yarns were undyed, or dyed with cochineal and vegetable colourants such as indigo. 98″ × 51″ (248.9 × 129.5 cm). Collection Michael Caden.*

PLATE 3

Late nineteenth-century tapestry-woven sarape *from Oaxaca. Examples of this style and period are described as 'transitional Saltillo'. Woollen weft yarns were dyed with aniline colourants. 100″ × 50″ (254 × 127 cm). Collection Michael Caden.*

PLATE 4

Nineteenth-century two-web sarape *with a cotton weft and a wool warp. Tapestry-woven on a treadle loom, it features an aggregate-diamond centre. 6'2" × 3'5" (188 × 104 cm). Maudslay Bequest. Victoria and Albert Museum, London.*

PLATE 5

Nineteenth-century two-web **sarape**. *Tapestry-woven on a treadle loom with a cotton warp and a wool weft, it is edged with red silk braid. Small diamonds and diagonal parallelograms form vertical bands round the serrated concentric diamond centre. 89″ × 49″ (225.5 × 124.5 cm). Maudslay Bequest. Victoria and Albert Museum, London.*

PLATE 6

Late transitional tapestry-woven silk and wool sarape, *c. 1920. Colours were achieved with aniline dyes. Designs are simpler than formerly. 81" × 38" (205.7 × 96.5 cm). Collection Michael Caden.*

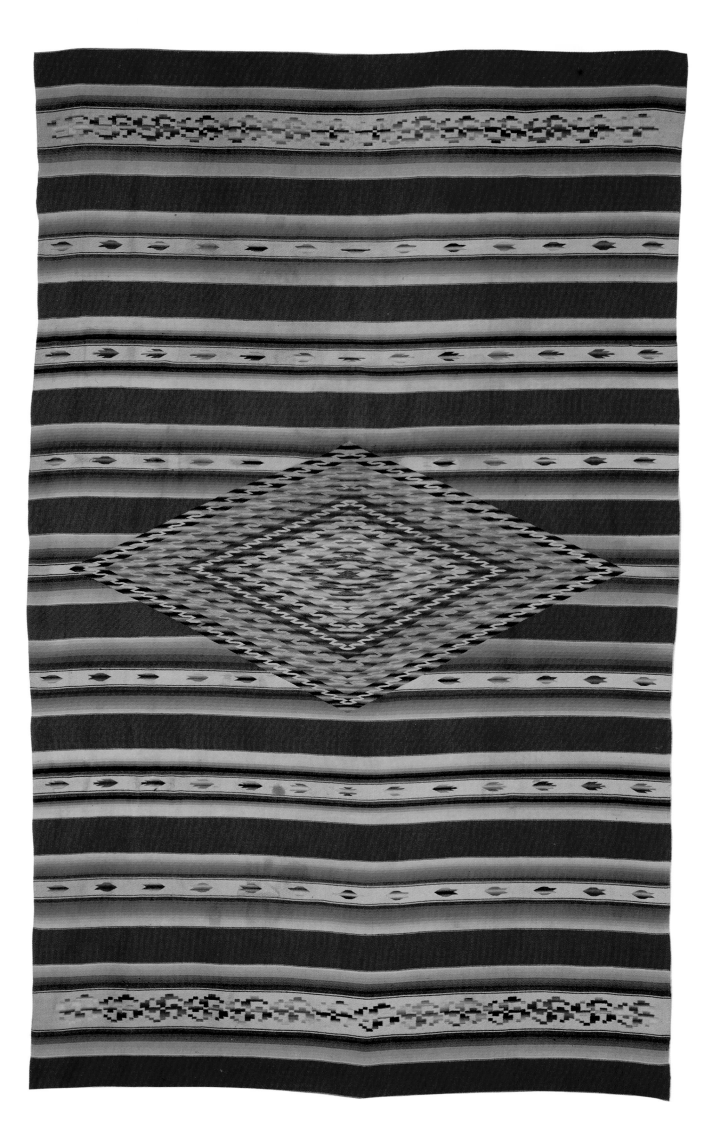

PLATES 7a, 7b

End sections of a linen rebozo, *or rectangular shawl, c. 1750. (The middle section is shown in Plate 8.) The ground is divided horizontally into three main bands, enclosed by geometrically patterned borders. Silk-embroidered motifs include figures in contemporary costume, fountains and other Mexico City landmarks. The bottom band is thought to show the famous floating gardens of Xochimilco. Height of sections (i.e. shawl width): 28½" (72.4 cm). Total length of shawl: 87" (221 cm). Parham Park, West Sussex.*

a

b

PLATE 8

Middle section of a mid-eighteenth-century rebozo, *or rectangular shawl, depicting life in Mexico City. (The end sections are shown in Plate 7.) Silk-embroidered designs include fountains, coaches and riders on horseback. Imported textiles from Imperial China almost certainly influenced needlework design during this period. Height (i.e. shawl width): 28½" (72.4 cm). Total length of shawl: 87" (221 cm). Parham Park, West Sussex.*

PLATE 9

Late eighteenth-century linen sampler embroidered with silver-gilt thread, purl, spangles and coloured silks. French knots, long and short, satin and stem stitching have been used. Designs suggest European and Oriental influence. 12" × 15¼" (30.5 × 39.4 cm). Victoria and Albert Museum, London.

PLATE 10

Section of a nineteenth-century linen altar cloth featuring deshilado, *or drawn threadwork. Motifs include crosses, sacred hearts, lions, monkeys, squirrels and birds. 67¼" × 23¼" (171 × 59 cm). Maudslay Bequest. Victoria and Albert Museum, London.*

PLATE 11

Linen sampler embroidered before 1911 in pattern darning stitch with blue silk. Zoomorphic designs include double-headed eagles with crowns, once the emblem of the House of Habsburg. 19" × 16½" (48.2 × 41.9 cm). Victoria and Albert Museum, London.

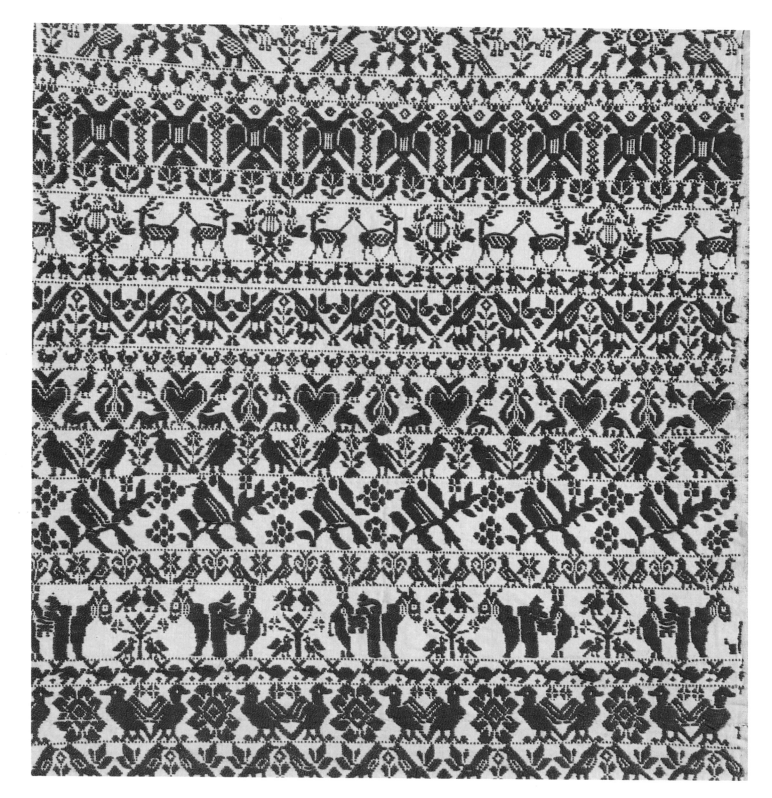

PLATE 12

Nineteenth-century huipil, *or woman's tunic, made from a single web of cotton cloth. Plain and gauze-woven on the backstrap loom, it features a wealth of embroidered decoration. Although there is no record of its place of origin, its similarity with the garment shown in Plate 88 suggests that it, too, is from the Mazatec village of Ayautla in the State of Oaxaca. 35½" × 33" (90.2 × 83.8 cm). Victoria and Albert Museum, London.*

PLATE 13

Contemporary ikat-*patterned* rebozo, *or rectangular shawl, from Toluca in the State of Mexico. Woven on a backstrap loom, this style of* rebozo *is known locally as a rebozo de* bola, *because it requires exactly one* bola, *or ball, of cotton. Before immersing her warp threads in aniline dye, the weaver has bound them at pre-determined intervals. Width of area shown: 14" (35.7 cm). Collection Chloë Sayer.*

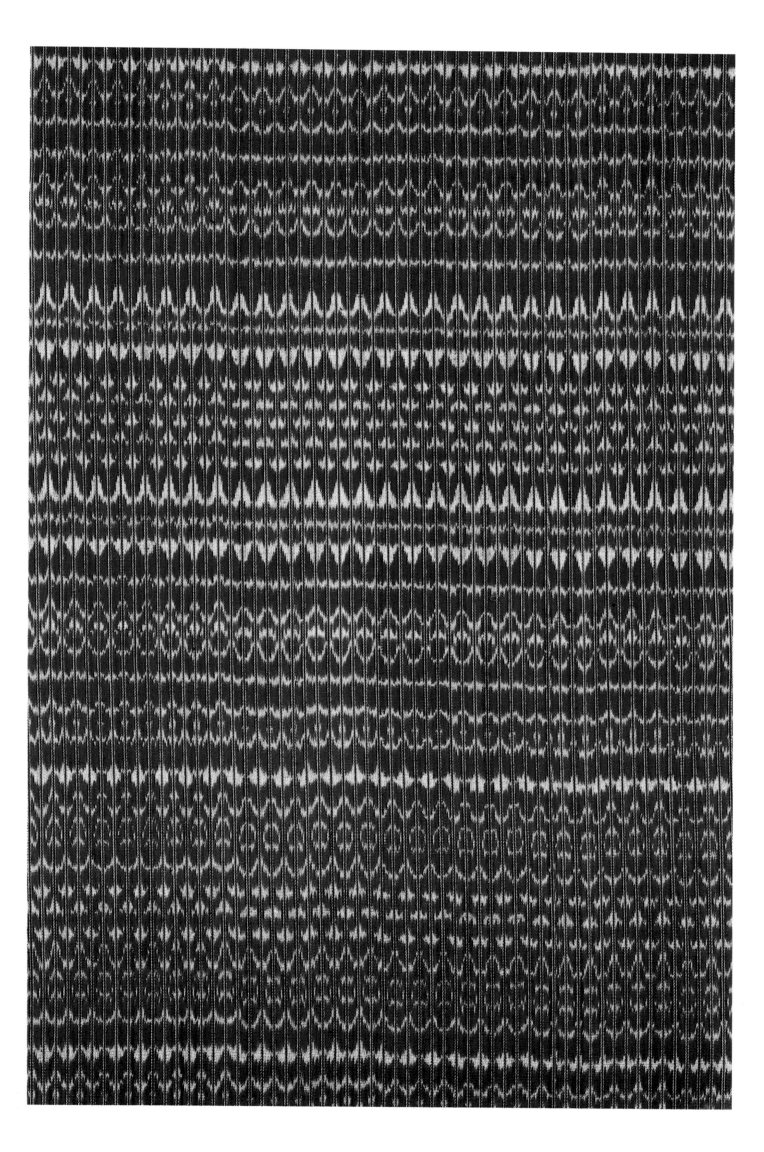

PLATE 14

Contemporary ikat-*patterned* rebozo, *or rectangular shawl, of several colours. Woven from artificial silk on a backstrap loom in Santa María del Río, San Luis Potosí, it features warp bands of patterning. Eighteenth- and nineteenth-century shawls were often decorated in this way. Width of area shown: 14" (35.7 cm). Collection Chloë Sayer.*

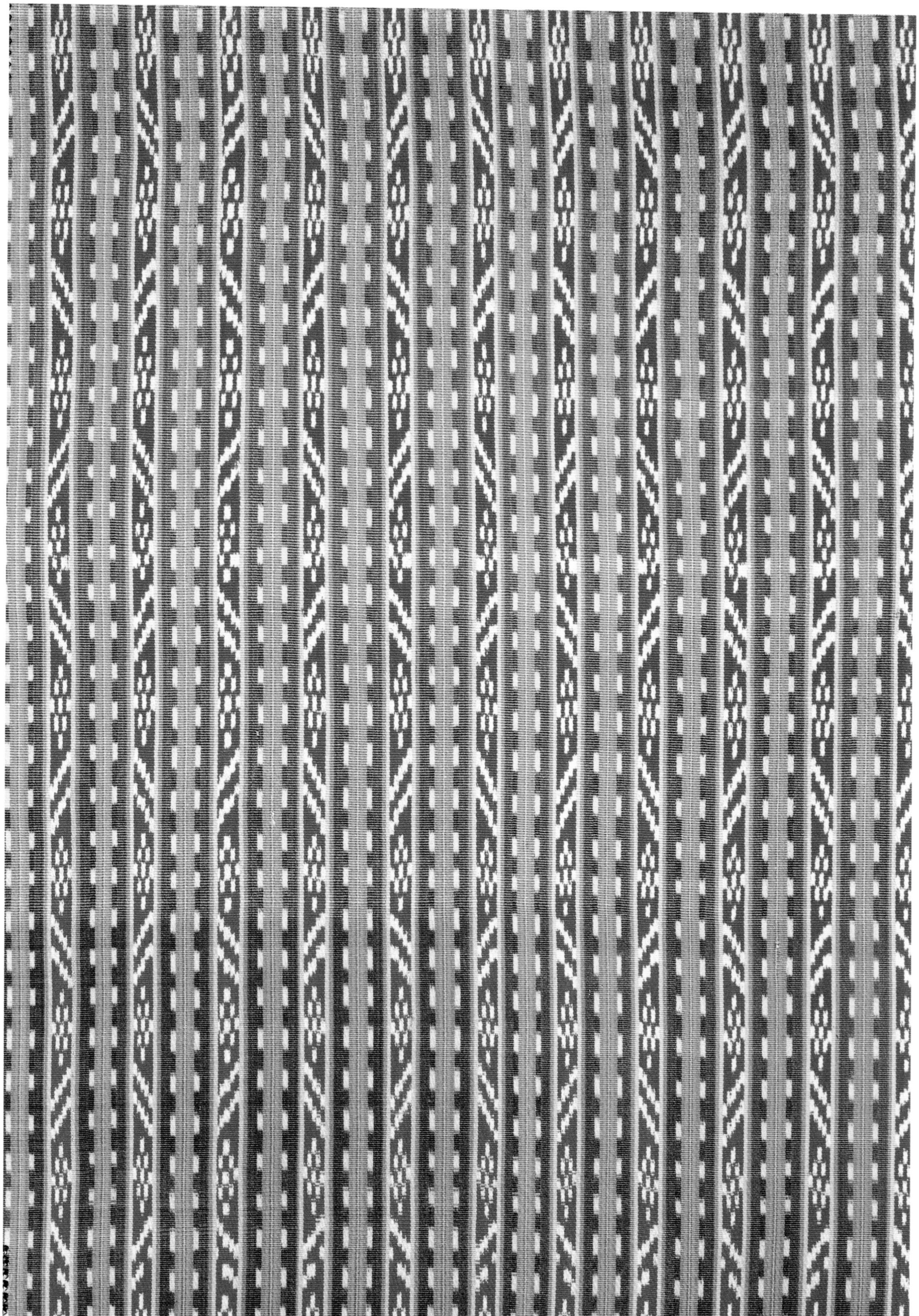

PLATE 15

Contemporary tapestry-patterned sarape *from Coatepec Harinas in the State of Mexico. Woven on a treadle loom from undyed wool of various shades, it features a wealth of interlocking geometric designs. These include cruciform motifs and stars with eight points. 67½" × 38½" (171.5 × 97.8 cm). Collection Camilla Hasse.*

PLATES 16a, 16b

Embroidered Otomí blouse strips from San Pablito, Puebla. Zoomorphic and anthropomorphic designs are worked in cross stitch and long-armed cross stitch on open-meshed commercial cotton cloth. Characteristically, the bodies of animals are filled in with squares or double spiral (ilhuitl) motifs. Although acrylic yarns have been used, the quality of the embroidery is extremely fine. Other pattern elements include diminutive eight-point stars or flowers. Width of yokes: 12½" (31.8 cm). Collection Chloë Sayer.

a

b

PLATES 17a, 17b

Beaded blouse panels from the Otomí village of San Pablito, Puebla. Sewn down one by one on to open-meshed commercial cloth, the glass beads form bird and animal designs. Such blouses are occasionally worn by Otomí women during festivals; more often, however, they are made for sale to outsiders. For 17a, width of beaded neck area: 13½" (34.3 cm). Museum of Mankind, London. For 17b, height of beaded sleeve area: 6¼" (15.9 cm). Collection Camilla Hasse.

a

b

PLATE 18

Embroidered section of a woman's quechquemitl, *or closed shoulder-cape, from San Pablito, Puebla. In this Otomí village embroidered* quechquemitl *are of two types — the other is shown in Plate 19. Motifs have been worked with acrylic yarn in cross stitch, long-armed cross stitch and outline stitch on open-meshed commercial cloth. Design elements include a human figure, a rearing horse and several birds. The double-headed eagle appears on a number of textiles throughout Mexico. Area shown: 10½" × 19" (26.5 × 48.3 cm). Collection Chloë Sayer.*

PLATE 19

Embroidered section of a woman's quechquemitl, *or closed shoulder-cape, from San Pablito, Puebla. In this Otomí village embroidered* quechquemitl *are of two types — the other is shown in Plate 18. Motifs have been worked with acrylic yarn in cross stitch and long-armed cross stitch on a plain-woven ground. Pattern elements are arranged bilaterally. The popular eight-point star or flower motif is rendered in several ways; sections contain birds and ancient designs. These include S-shapes and stepped-fret patterning. Area shown 11¼" × 12" (28.6 × 30.5 cm). Collection Chloë Sayer.*

PLATE 20

Embroidered wall-hanging of commercial cotton cloth from the Otomí village of San Pablito, Puebla. Worked in surface satin stitch with acrylic yarn, designs include turkeys, butterflies, fish and a host of other creatures grouped round the national emblem of Mexico — an eagle perched on a prickly pear with a serpent in its beak. 72" × 75" (183 × 190 cm). Collection Chloë Sayer.

PLATE 21

Embroidered wall-hanging of commercial cotton cloth from the Otomí community of Tenango de Doria, Hidalgo. Worked in surface satin stitch with commercial cotton thread, it shows devils and angels dancing round the sun. 62" × 74¾" (157.5 × 189.8 cm). Museum of Mankind, London.

PLATE 22

Embroidered servilleta *of commercial cotton cloth from the Otomí village of Santa Monica, Puebla. Worked in surface satin stitch with commercial cotton thread, it shows an armadillo surrounded by leaves and flowers. 12½" × 17¼" (31.8 × 43.8 cm). Collection Chloë Sayer.*

PLATES 23a, 23b

Otomí shoulder-bags from El Progreso in the Mezquital Valley, Hidalgo. Cloth is double-woven on the backstrap loom with cotton and acrylic yarn. Bag (a) features flowers and a goat. Width: 10" (26.7 cm). Bag (b) shows an eagle perched on a prickly pear cactus with a serpent in its beak; this is the national emblem of Mexico. Width: 12" (30.5 cm). Collection Chloë Sayer.

a

b

PLATE 24a

Otomí shoulder-bag. Cloth is double-woven on the backstrap loom with undyed wool to show a horse with a plumed tail. 12½" × 15½" (31.8 × 39.4 cm). Collection Chloë Sayer.

PLATE 24b

Otomí sash from the Ixmiquilpan region of Hidalgo. Woven on the backstrap loom from commercial cotton thread, it displays warp patterning. Area shown: 5" × 7" (12.7 × 17.8 cm). Collection Chloë Sayer.

a

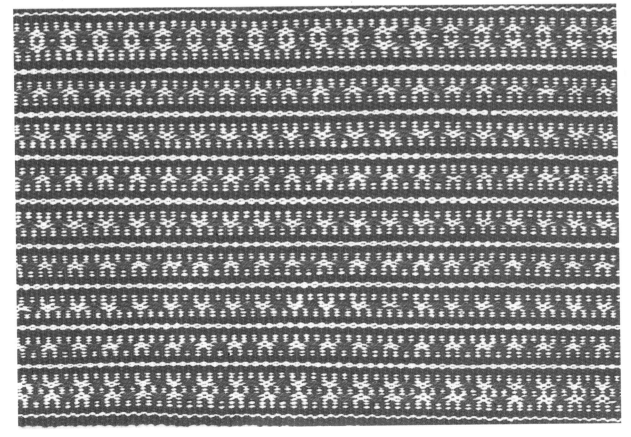

b

PLATE 25

Otomí woman's waist-sash from Santiago Mezquititlan, Querétaro. Shown here in three sections, it was plain-woven from cotton on the backstrap loom by Josefa Francisco Ventura. Woven designs, worked with acrylic warp yarns, include brocaded animals, birds and flowers. Width: 2½" (6.3 cm). Museum of Mankind, London.

PLATES 26a, 26b

Otomí waist-sashes for women from Tixmadeje in the State of Mexico. Plain-woven from cotton on the backstrap loom by Regina Álvarez, they feature brocaded designs worked with a wool warp. Superstructural patterns include bird, animal, plant and geometric motifs. Approximate height (i.e. width of sashes): 3½" (8.9 cm). Museum of Mankind, London.

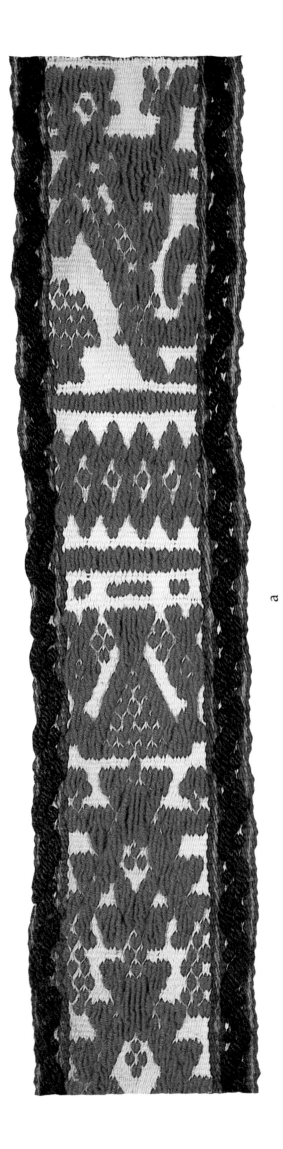

a

b

PLATE 27

Four-web bedspread made by Otomí weaver Ana Cecilia Cruz Alberto of San Miguel Ameyalco in the State of Mexico. Woven on a backstrap loom from white commercial cotton, it features a profusion of designs; these include such non-indigenous elements as churches and horses. Created on the loom, designs are brocaded on the plain-woven ground with brightly coloured acrylic yarns. 73½" × 101" (186.7 × 256.5 cm). Museum of Mankind, London.

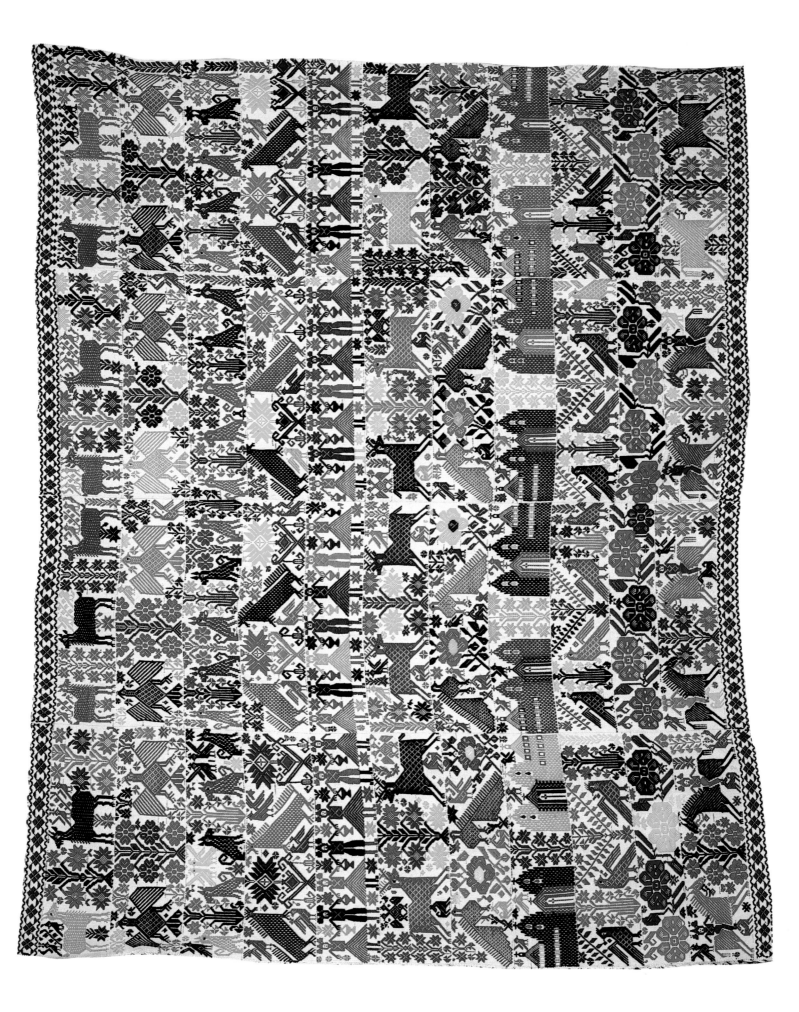

PLATES 28a, 28b

Embroidered Otomí blouse strips from Santa Ana Hueytlalpan, Hidalgo. Worked in cross stitch by Narda Flores Cruz, they feature concentric diamonds with a serrated outer edge, and eight-petal flowers. In recent years blouses have become increasingly ornate and brilliantly coloured. These examples are for everyday use; gala examples often include silver braid and sequins. Approximate width of area shown: 10" (25.4 cm). Museum of Mankind, London.

a

b

PLATE 29

Man's shoulder-bag of commercial cotton cloth from the Otomí village of Santa Monica, situated on the borderline between the states of Puebla and Hidalgo. Cross-stitched with the owner's name, the bag also displays bird motifs. The double-headed eagle in the centre is filled in with animal designs and a four-point star. 11½" (29.2 cm) square. Museum of Mankind, London.

PLATE 30a

Embroidered Otomí blouse strips from San Pablito, Puebla. Cockerels and smaller birds are embroidered in pattern running stitch with commercial cotton thread. Width of area shown: 14" (35.5 cm). Museum of Mankind, London.

PLATE 30b

Mazahua skirt border from the Toluca region of Mexico State. Highly stylized motifs, which include birds, people and deer, adorn the area shown. Embroidered chiefly in herringbone stitch, they are worked with acrylic yarns on commercial cotton cloth. Height of embroidered section: 7¼" (18.4 cm). Collection Chloë Sayer.

a

b

PLATE 31a

Flower and leaf designs, embroidered with acrylic yarns, embellish this fringed Mazahua quechquemitl, *or closed shoulder-cape, from Santa Ana Eyenzú in the State of Mexico. The background cloth was plain-woven from wool on a backstrap loom; white cotton warp threads provide narrow lines of patterning. The Mazahua specialize in crossed stitches; this garment is chiefly embellished in herringbone stitch. Width of webs (excluding fringe): 10¾" (27.3 cm). Collection Camilla Hasse.*

PLATE 31b

Embroidered quechquemitl, *or closed shoulder-cape, from the Mazahua village of San Francisco Tepeolulco in the State of Mexico. The background cloth was plain-woven from wool and acrylic yarn on a backstrap loom; by moving occasional pink warp threads, the weaver has created thin zig-zag lines. Flower, plant and bird motifs are worked with acrylic yarn; herringbone is the principal stitch used. This* quechquemitl *was made in the early 1980s; subsequent years have seen a vogue for increased decoration (see Plate 31). Width of webs (excluding the fringe, which is not shown): 12" (30.5 cm). Museum of Mankind, London.*

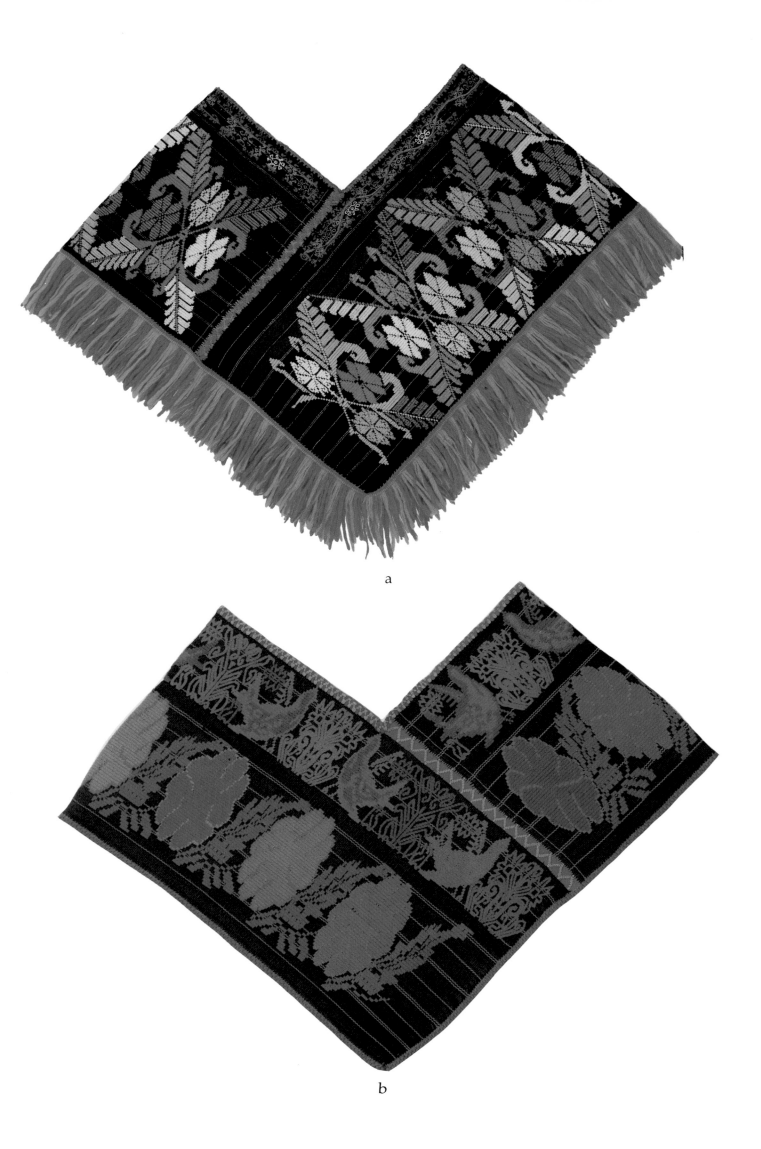

a

b

PLATE 32

Densely embroidered section of a Mazahua woman's quechquemitl, *or closed shoulder-cape, from San Francisco Tepeolulco in the State of Mexico. Although barely visible, the background cloth was plain-woven from cotton and acrylic thread; 'floating' warp threads provide thin green lines of zig-zag patterning. Three horizontal bands contain embroidered birds, deer and flower designs worked chiefly in herringbone stitch with acrylic yarns. Made in 1988 by Teresa Sánchez Galindo, it is more richly decorated than earlier examples (see Plate 31b). Approximate width of area shown: 17" (43.1 cm). Museum of Mankind, London.*

PLATES 33a, 33b

Woven sashes remain one of the richest design sources. This much-worn example is shown in two sections. From the Mazahua community of San Simón de la Laguna in the State of Mexico, it displays a wealth of patterning. Bird, animal and plant motifs are warp-brocaded with black and blue wool over a plain-woven cotton ground. Height (i.e. width of sash): 3½" (8.9 cm). Museum of Mankind, London.

a

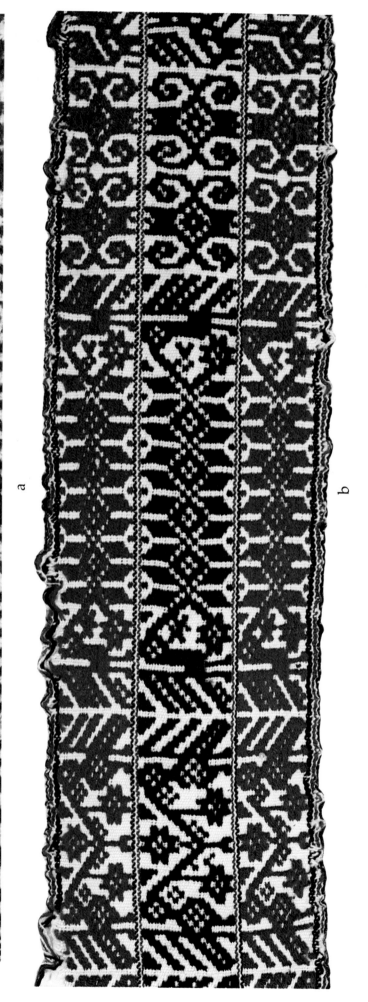

b

PLATES 34a, 34b

Two details from the same Mazahua skirt border. Using cross stitch, long-armed cross stitch and herringbone stitch, women in San Simón de la Laguna, Mexico State, pattern skirts and servilletas. Designs are embroidered with acrylic yarns on to open-meshed commercial cloth. Highly stylized animals and flowers combine with interlocking geometric designs. Height of border: 6½" (16.5 cm). Collection Chloë Sayer.

a

b

PLATE 35a

Mazahua woman's sash of cotton and acrylic from Pueblo Nuevo in the State of Mexico. Warp-brocaded designs include flowers set within zig-zag lines. Height (i.e. width of sash): 4" (10.2 cm). Museum of Mankind, London.

PLATE 35b

The Mazahua women of San Simón de la Laguna in the State of Mexico are skilled weavers. This waist-sash displays a range of stylized flower, bird and animal motifs. Warp-brocaded in wool on a plain-woven cotton ground, they recall pre-Hispanic designs. Height (i.e. width of sash): 5¼" (13.3 cm). Collection Chloë Sayer.

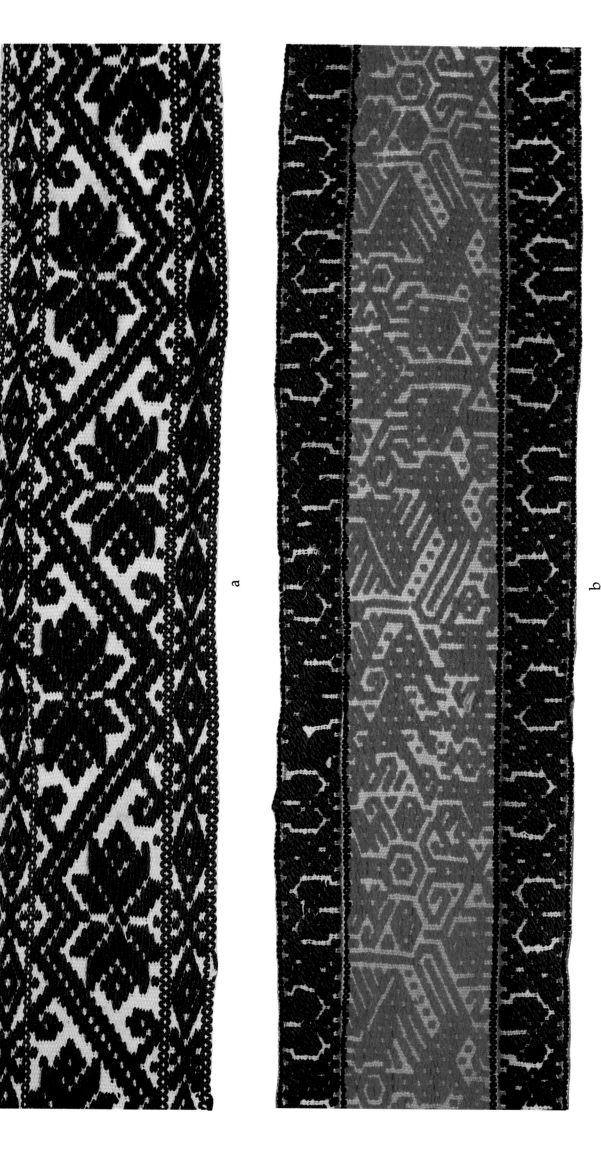

a

b

PLATE 36a

Detail from a Mazahua shoulder-bag of cotton and wool. Woven on a backstrap loom near Villa de Allende in the State of Mexico, it features dense embroidery done with cross stitch, long-armed cross stitch and herringbone stitch. Width of embroidered section: 5¾" (14.6 cm). Collection Chloë Sayer.

PLATE 36b

Mazahua woman's sash from San Francisco Tepeolulco in the State of Mexico. Woven on a backstrap loom, it features warp-brocaded animals worked with wool on a plain-woven cotton and wool background. Height (i.e. width of sash): 3¼" (8.3 cm). Museum of Mankind, London.

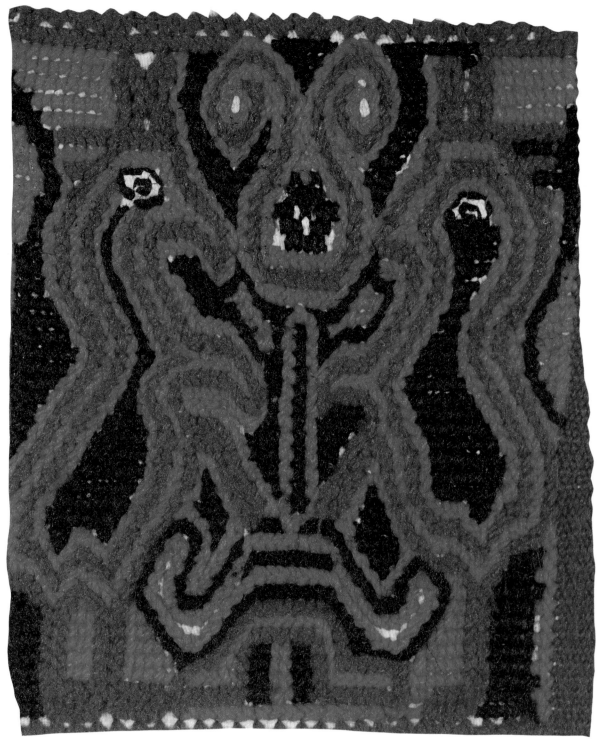

a

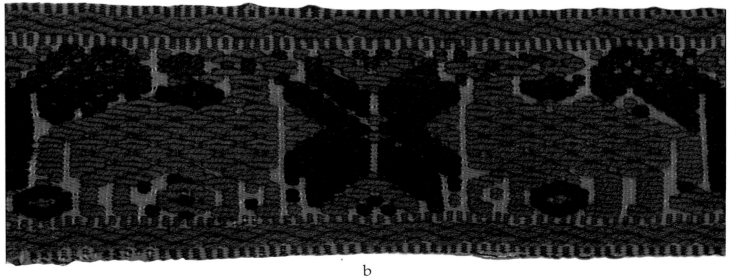

b

PLATE 37a

Mazahua woman's sash of cotton and wool from San Felipe Santiago in the State of Mexico. Warp-brocaded designs, which include animals and flowers, are repeated along the length of the sash. Height (i.e. width of sash): 3¼" (8.3 cm). Museum of Mankind, London.

PLATE 37b

Woman's warp-brocaded sash of wool and cotton from the Mazahua community of San Simón de la Laguna in the State of Mexico. Because prolonged use has felted the raised designs on the right side, they are seen here in the negative on the reverse side. The two central animals recall pre-Hispanic jaguars portrayed at Tula and other archaeological sites. Height (i.e. width of sash): 4" (10.2 cm). Collection Chloë Sayer.

PLATE 37c

San Simón de la Laguna in the State of Mexico is one of a decreasing number of villages where small girls still wear indigenous clothing. Woven on a backstrap loom, this Mazahua child's sash features a multitude of birds and animals. These are warp-brocaded with wool on a plain-woven cotton ground. Height (i.e. width of sash): 2¾" (7 cm). Museum of Mankind, London.

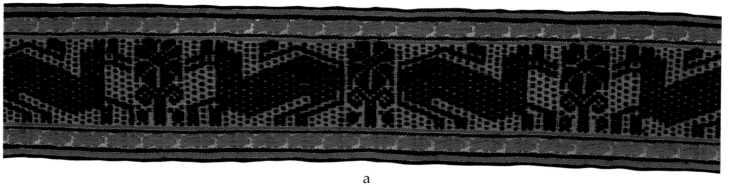

a

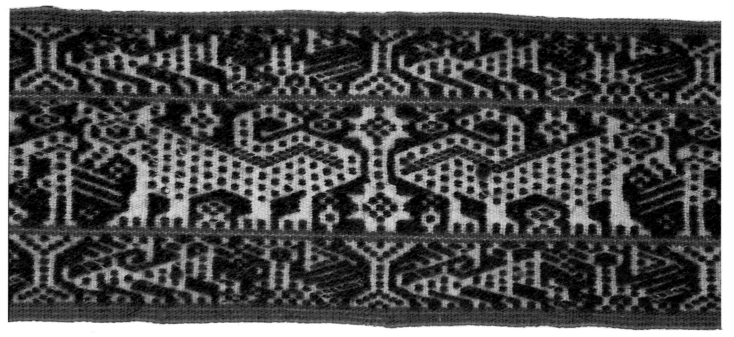

b

c

PLATE 38a

Central blouse area. Woven from black wool in the Nahua village of Hueyapan, Puebla, it shows a pot of flowers with stylized branches, surrounded by birds; two rabbits are portrayed underneath. Motifs are cross-stitched with wool yarn. Approximate height of area shown: 13" (33 cm). Museum of Mankind, London.

PLATE 38b

Mazahua woman's sash from San Francisco Tepeolulco in the State of Mexico. Woven on a backstrap loom, it features warp-brocaded patterning worked with acrylic yarns on a plain-woven cotton background. Height (i.e. width of sash): 3" (7.6 cm). Museum of Mankind, London.

a

b

PLATES 39a, 39b, 39c

*Nahua blouse strips of factory-produced cotton cloth from Alaxtitla
Poxtectitla and Ixcacuatitla, Veracruz. Indian women in this region are
skilled in the art of cross stitch. Sleeves and yokes are densely patterned
with parrots (top), flowers (middle) and cockerels (below). These are worked
with commercial cotton thread. Average height of yoke: 4½" (11.4 cm).
Collection Chloë Sayer.*

a

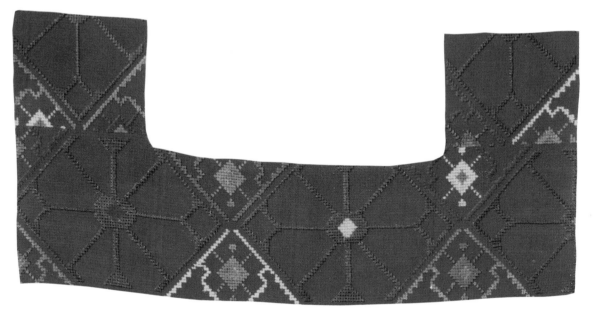

b

c

PLATE 40a, 40b

Blouse strips of commercial cotton cloth from the Nahua village of Huilacapixtla, Puebla. Designs are embroidered in pattern running stitch with acrylic yarn. Throughout this region decorative panels are often sold to local women who are unable or unwilling to embroider their own blouses. Width of neckband: 13½″ (34.3 cm). Collection Chloë Sayer.

a

b

PLATES 41a, 41b

Front and back view of a Nahua blouse from Xaltepec, Puebla. One side (a) shows a heart surrounded by flowers and the Spanish word for heart (corazón), the other (b) features stylized peacocks and flowers. These designs are worked on commercial cotton cloth in pattern running stitch. Although the work is crudely executed with thick acrylic yarn, the effect is pleasing. Height of embroidered sections: 10" (25.4 cm). Collection Chloë Sayer.

a

b

PLATE 42a

Blouse yoke of commercial cotton cloth, embroidered by María Antonia Martes in the Nahua village of Huilacapixtla, Puebla. The deer and surrounding designs are worked in pattern running stitch with green wool. Tiny elements of negative patterning embellish the body of the deer. Height: 6" (15.2 cm). Museum of Mankind, London.

PLATE 42b

Blouse yoke of commercial cotton cloth from the Nahua village of Chachahuantla, Puebla. The deer and surrounding designs are embroidered by hand in pattern running stitch with commercial cotton thread. Height: 6" (15.2 cm). Collection Chloë Sayer.

a

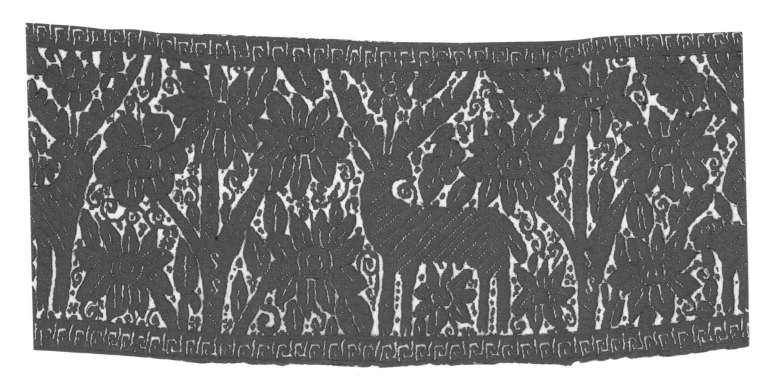

b

PLATE 43a

Nahua blouse strips, embroidered with commercial cotton thread by Cecilia Vargas of Atla, Puebla. The yoke is worked by hand in pattern running stitch; designs include squirrels, S-shaped motifs and zig-zag lines. Sleeve bands are machine-embroidered. Width of area shown: 13½" (34.3 cm). Museum of Mankind, London.

PLATE 43b

Nahua blouse strips of open-meshed commercial cotton cloth from Xaltepec, Puebla. The yoke is hand-embroidered in acrylic yarn with pattern running stitch to show a goat with flower vases. Width of area shown: 12¾" (32.4 cm). Museum of Mankind, London.

a

b

PLATES 44a, 44b

Front and back panels of a Nahua blouse from Coacuila, Puebla. Both sides display images of the Virgin Mary, surrounded by birds, flowers, cherubs and decorative lettering. The front view (a) shows the Virgin of Guadalupe, Patron Saint of Mexico. Motifs are worked in pattern running stitch; background cloth and cotton embroidery threads were commercially produced. Height of panels: 8½" (21.6 cm). Collection Chloë Sayer.

a

b

PLATES 45a, 45b

Blouse strips of commercial cotton cloth from the Nahua village of Atla, Puebla. Zoomorphic and anthropomorphic motifs are achieved with the aid of pattern running stitches which create areas of negative patterning. Known as **pepenado**, *this technique is becoming rare. Approximate height of panels: 4¼" (10.8 cm). Collection Chloë Sayer and Museum of Mankind, London.*

a b

PLATES 46a, 46b

Nahua blouse strips, embroidered in pattern running stitch, from the Cuetzalan region, Puebla. Worked on commercial cotton cloth with cotton and artificial silk threads, they show dogs (a) and horses with plumed tails (b) surrounded by a variety of other motifs. Height 3½" (8.9 cm). Collection Chloë Sayer.

a

b

PLATE 47

Nahua blouse strips of commercial cotton cloth, sold to local women in the market of Atlixco, Veracruz. Designs are embroidered in pattern running stitch. They include eight-petal flowers, inset with S-shaped motifs (ilhuitl) and hooked motifs. Although acrylic yarns have been used, the patterning is bold and pleasing. Width of neckband: 13½" (34.3 cm). Collection Chloë Sayer.

Details taken from an embroidered quechquemitl *from the Nahua village of Santa Catarina, Puebla. Cross-stitched patterning on commercially produced cotton cloth includes eight-point stars and eight-petal flowers; these may be filled in with tiny birds or with S-shaped motifs and spirals which echo the ancient* ilhuitl *design. Similar decorative elements occur in the neighbouring Otomí village of San Pablito (see Plate 19). Also shown are variations on the tree of life motif (see also Plate 37a). Approximate width of areas shown: (a) 18″ (45.7 cm), (b) 12″ (30.5 cm). Museum of Mankind, London.*

a

b

PLATE 49

Embroidered quechquemitl *section from the Nahua village of Santa Catarina, Puebla. Designs are worked with cotton thread and acrylic yarn in cross stitch and pattern running stitch on square-meshed factory cloth. Decorative elements include eight-point stars, eight-petal flowers, X-shaped motifs, birds, a double-headed eagle, a horse filled in with squares, and a plant growing out of a pot. Garments like this one are sometimes worn before the embroidery is completed; from time to time the owner will add further embellishments or finish existing motifs. Area shown: 11" × 20" (27.9 × 50.9 cm). Museum of Mankind, London.*

PLATES 50a, 50b

Details taken from a Nahua quechquemitl *from San Pedro Coyutla, Veracruz. Woven on a backstrap loom, it features raised weft-brocaded designs in bands. Other motifs are worked in cross-stitch. These include lions with flowers on their heads (a), and a basket of flowers (b). Designs, whether woven or embroidered, are achieved with red and black wool. San Pedro Coyutla is one of a small number of villages where women wear the* quechquemitl *without a blouse underneath. Width of areas shown: (a) 13" (33 cm), (b) 17" (43.2 cm). Museum of Mankind, London.*

a

b

PLATE 51a

Embroidered blouse strip from the Nahua village of Chachahuantla, Puebla. Deer and floral motifs are satin stitched with thick acrylic yarn. Width of area shown: 13½" (34.3 cm). Museum of Mankind, London.

PLATE 51b

Decorative band from a gauze-woven quechquemitl. *Made in the Nahua village of Atla, it features angular spirals worked with acrylic yarn. Despite appearances, designs were embroidered, not weft-brocaded. Width of area shown: 17" (43.2 cm). Museum of Mankind, London.*

a

b

PLATE 52a

Nahua woman's extremely fine weft-brocaded cotton sash from the Zongolica mountains of Veracruz. Motifs, worked on a plain-woven ground, are highly stylized. They represent a comb, a pathway and various plant species. Width of sash: 3" (8 cm). Collection Chloë Sayer.

PLATE 52b

Detail from an all-white quechquemitl *made in the Nahua village of Xolotla, Puebla. Woven on the backstrap loom from commercial cotton thread, it features motifs of figured gauze. These include deer and double-headed eagles. Width of area shown: 10" (25.7 cm). Museum of Mankind, London.*

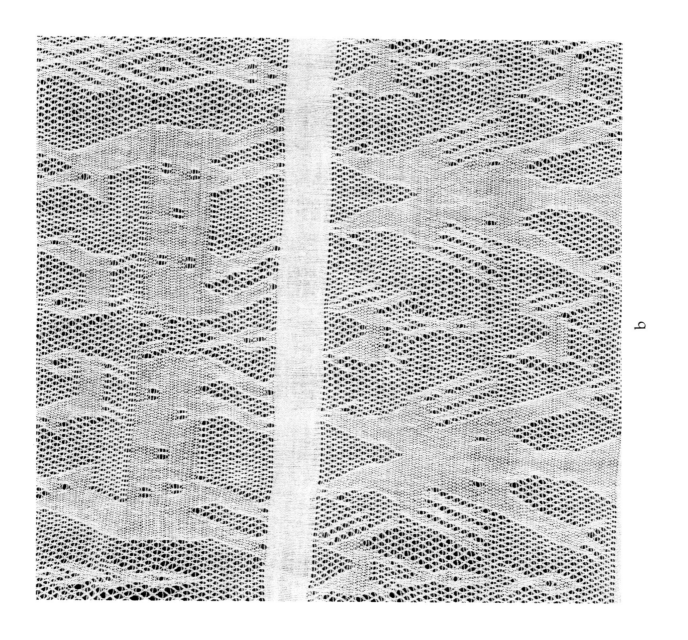

b

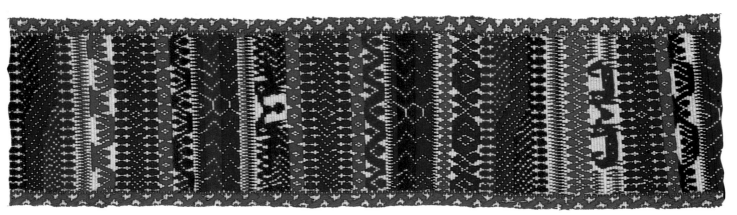

a

PLATE 53

Section of a woman's wrap-around skirt from the Nahua community of Acatlán, Guerrero. Plain-woven in two webs on a backstrap loom from indigo-dyed cotton, it features a wealth of embroidered designs worked with synthetic silk threads. Stitches include stem, fishbone and couching. Fanciful animals, birds and flowers abound; also shown is Mexico's national emblem (an eagle perched on a prickly pear, with a serpent in its beak). Area shown: 38" × 44½" (96.5 × 113 cm). Museum of Mankind, London.

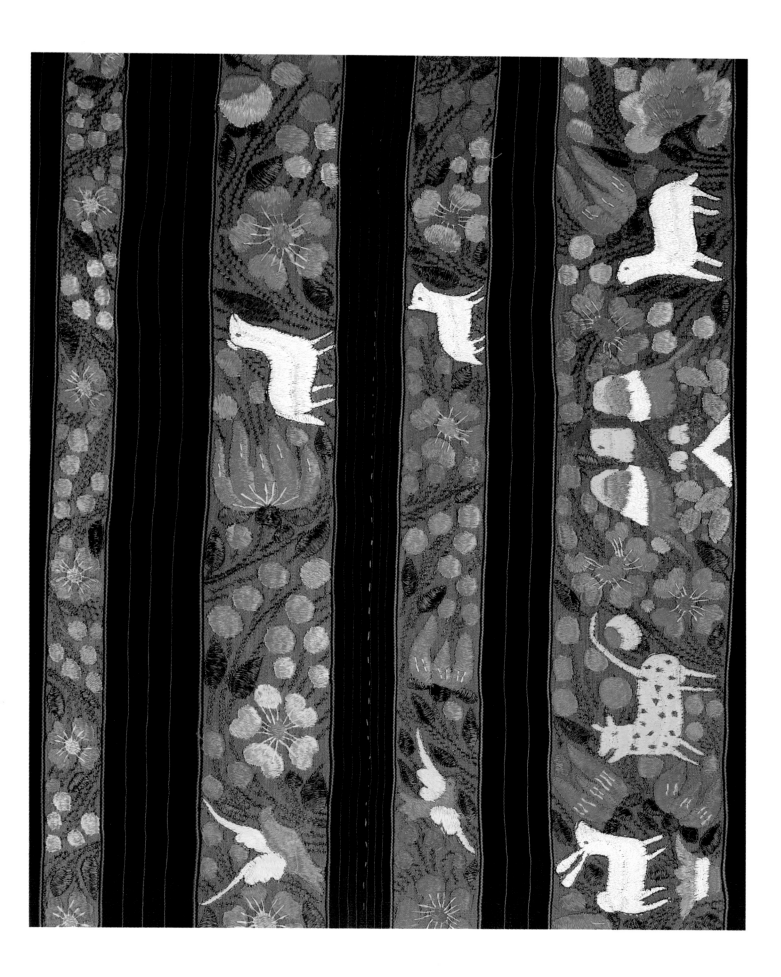

PLATE 54

Shoulder area of a gala huipil, *or woman's tunic, from the Nahua community of Acatlán, Guerrero. Made from commercial rayon, this garment is embellished with a profusion of flowers and birds. These are worked with glistening synthetic silk threads. Stitches include long-armed cross, fishbone and stem. Width of area shown: 12" (35 cm). Collection Chloë Sayer.*

PLATE 55a

*Nahua woman's warp-patterned sash from the Cuetzalan region of Puebla.
Woven on a backstrap loom from cotton and wool, it features warp stripes.
Width of sash: 5¼" (13.3 cm). Collection Chloë Sayer.*

PLATE 55b

Fringed Huastec quechquemitl, *or closed shoulder-cape, from the
Tancanhuitz region of San Luis Potosí. Made from commercial cloth, it
features cross-stitched designs worked with commercial cotton thread and
some acrylic. These include stylized birds and animals, eight-point star or
flower motifs, and zig-zag lines. Double-headed eagles are also shown.
Width from corner to corner: 26¼" (66.7 cm). Collection Chloë Sayer.*

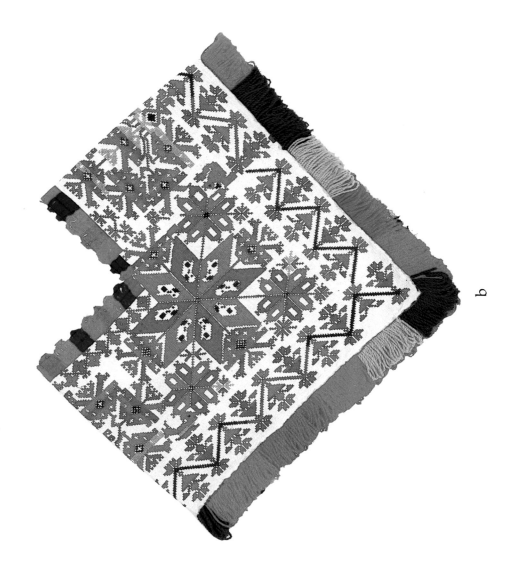

b

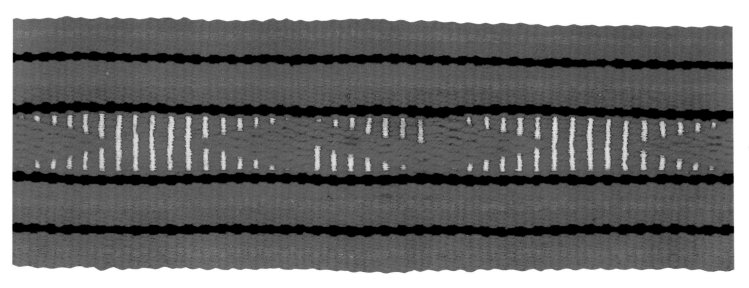

a

PLATE 56a

Huastec servilleta *from San Luis Potosí. Made from commercial cloth, it is decorated with formalized designs done in cross stitch with commercial cotton thread. These include crowned lions, once the emblem of the House of Habsburg. 14¾" × 21" (37.4 × 55.2 cm). Collection Chloë Sayer.*

PLATE 56b

Tepehua shoulder-bag of commercial cotton cloth. Geometric and eight-petal flower motifs are embroidered in pattern running stitch with cotton thread. 13¼" (33.7 cm) square. Collection Chloë Sayer.

a

b

PLATE 57a

Totonac blouse section, with an opening for the head, from the Papantla region of Veracruz. Flower and leaf motifs are embroidered on open-meshed commercial cloth with cross stitch and long-armed cross stitch. Although acrylic yarns have been used, the embroidery is finely done. Such designs show the influence of pattern sheets. 15½" × 13½" (39.3 × 34.4). Collection Chloë Sayer.

PLATE 57b

Embroidered kerchief section of commercial cloth from El Tajín, Veracruz. Kerchiefs are worn on festive occasions by Totonac men. Worked in satin stitch with commercial cotton thread by Fredy Mendez, it features glass studs; cut like diamonds, they glint in the sunlight. Width of area shown: 12½" (31.7 cm). Museum of Mankind, London.

a

b

PLATES 58a, 58b

The Huichol Indians live in one of the remotest areas of Mexico; this inhospitable and mountainous region stretches into the states of Jalisco, Nayarit, Durango and Zacatecas. Huichol women specialize in weaving double-cloth bags on the backstrap loom. Designs are extremely varied. Both sides of this double-woven bag are shown; they display bird and plant motifs, together with a spiral-patterned border at the top, worked with undyed wool. Height: 12½" (31.8 cm). Collection Chloë Sayer.

a

b

PLATE 59

Detail taken from a man's shoulder-bag of acrylic yarn from the Huichol area of Jalisco. Double-woven on a backstrap loom, it features animal motifs. Traditionally such bags were made with undyed wool, but acrylic yarns now inspire striking colour combinations. Width of area shown: 8" (20.3 cm). Collection Chloë Sayer.

PLATE 60a

*Man's shoulder-bag of acrylic yarn from the Huichol area of Jalisco.
Double-woven on a backstrap loom, it features deer and other zoomorphic
motifs. Area shown: approximately 9½" (22.8 cm) square. Collection
Chloë Sayer.*

PLATE 60b

*Man's shoulder-bag of acrylic yarn from the Huichol area of Jalisco.
Double-woven on a backstrap loom, it shows turkeys and flowers. Area
shown: approximately 10" (25.4 cm) square. Collection Chloë Sayer.*

a

b

PLATES 61a, 61b

Two sides, with varying designs, of a Huichol man's shoulder-bag from Jalisco. Double-woven on a backstrap loom, it combines wool and acrylic yarn. 10" × 10½" (25.4 × 26.7 cm). Collection Chloë Sayer.

a

b

PLATES 62a, 62b

*Huichol shoulder-bags of wool and acrylic yarn. Double-woven on a
backstrap loom, they display cockerels (a) and eight-petal flowers (b). 62a is
12" (35 cm) square. Museum of Mankind, London. 62b is 7" × 9" (17.7 ×
22.8 cm). Collection Chloë Sayer.*

a

b

PLATE 63a

Huichol man's shoulder-bag of netted beadwork with a cloth backing, from Jalisco. Tiny glass beads form eight-petal flowers and a vine motif. 6" (15.2 cm) square. Collection Chloë Sayer.

PLATE 63b

Huichol man's waist-sash of netted beadwork with a cloth backing, from Jalisco. Shown here in two sections, it is patterned with deer motifs. Height (i.e. width) of each section: 2" (5 cm). Museum of Mankind, London.

a

b

PLATE 64a

Huichol man's shirt of commercial cloth, decorated in cross stitch and long-armed cross stitch, from Jalisco. Huichol men are renowned for the splendour of their clothing. Here traditional stepped-fret designs are combined with figurative elements which probably derive from contemporary pattern sheets. Width of shirt: 17½" (44.4 cm). Collection Chloë Sayer.

PLATE 64b

Huichol man's trouser leg of commercial cloth from Jalisco. Worked with cotton thread in cross stitch and long-armed cross stitch, designs include horse-back riders and Aztec warriors; these were probably inspired by pattern sheets. The embroiderer has added simulated bead droplets. Height of area shown: 15½" (39.3 cm). Collection Chloë Sayer.

a

b

PLATES 65a, 65b

Huichol quechquemitl *from San Andrés Cohamiata, Jalisco. Cloth and cotton embroidery threads were commercially produced. Designs are worked in cross stitch, long-armed cross stitch and herringbone stitch. The* totó *flower, shown with eight petals, and the double-headed eagle are recurring motifs on Huichol textiles. S-shaped motifs recall pre-Hispanic styles of patterning. Approximately 23½" (59.7 cm) square. 65a: Collection Chloë Sayer. 65b: Museum of Mankind, London.*

a

b

PLATE 66a

Huichol cotton bag, embroidered in cross stitch and long-armed cross stitch with geometric and flower motifs. The white cloth contributes to the over-all design. 7½" (19 cm) square. Museum of Mankind, London.

PLATE 66b

Detail from a Huichol man's embroidered shirt of commercial cloth. Designs are worked with commercial cotton thread in cross stitch and long-armed cross stitch. The lower border consists of interlocking S-shaped motifs. Height of area shown: 5¼" (13.3 cm). Collection Chloë Sayer.

a

b

PLATE 67

Huichol cotton bag, embroidered in cross stitch and long-armed cross stitch with interlocking geometric motifs. The white cloth contributes to the over-all design. 9" (22.8 cm) square. Museum of Mankind, London.

PLATES 68a, 68b

Embroidered Huichol borders from a woman's skirt (a) and a man's shoulder-cape (b) from San Andrés Cohamiata, Jalisco. Decorative elements include eight-petal flowers, birds and a cat. Stepped-fret patterning recalls pre-Hispanic designs. Cross, long-armed cross and herringbone are the stitches used. Cloth and cotton threads were factory-made. Height of areas shown: (a) 10½″ (26.7 cm), (b) 7¾″ (19.7 cm). Collection Chloë Sayer.

a

b

PLATE 69

Huichol cotton bag, closely embroidered in cross stitch and long-armed cross stitch with interlocking geometric designs. Diamond-and-hook motifs predominate. 8" (21 cm) square. Collection Chloë Sayer.

PLATE 70

Tarahumara man's sash of hand-spun, undyed wool. Woven on a rigid log loom, it features warp-patterned geometric units. The sash is reversible: white areas become black ones on the opposite side, and vice versa. Height (i.e. width of sash): 4" (10.2 cm). Collection Chloë Sayer.

PLATE 71

Zapotec woman's sash from Santo Tomás Jalieza, Oaxaca. Shown here in three sections, it was woven on a backstrap loom with cotton thread of different thicknesses. Sashes from this village are worn in many areas of Oaxaca. Cloth is warp-patterned to display a range of predominantly zoomorphic designs, although one section shows a dancer wearing a plumed headdress. Width: 2" (5 cm). Collection Chloë Sayer.

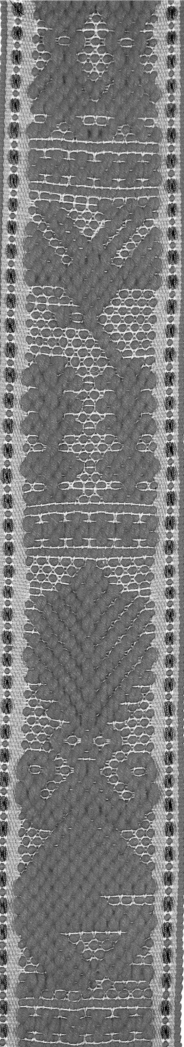

PLATES 72a, 72b

Cotton bags with warp patterning from the Zapotec village of Santo Tomás Jalieza, Oaxaca. Designs include humming birds taking nectar from flowers. For both bags, height: 7½" (19 cm), width: 5" (12.7 cm). Collection Chloë Sayer.

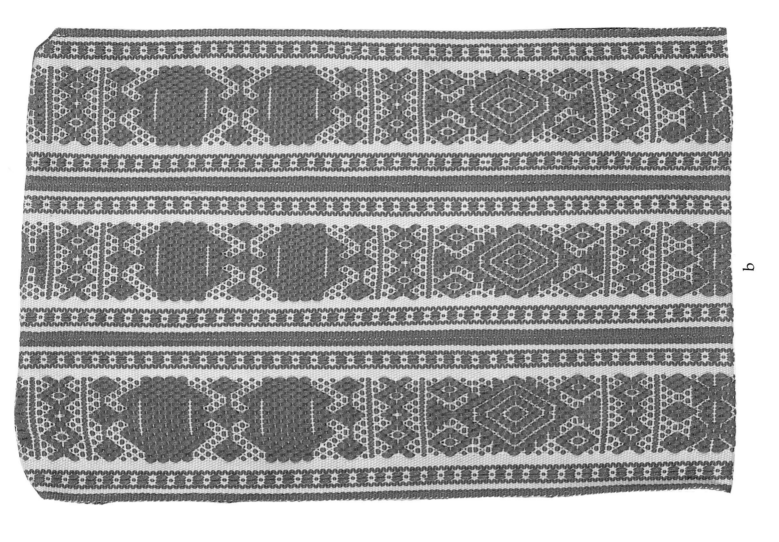

b

a

PLATE 73

Blouse sleeve from San Juan Chilateca, Oaxaca. Exquisitely embroidered by Faustina Sumano de Sánchez, it features satin-stitched flowers worked in silk. It is shown here at several times its actual size. Height of area shown: 6″ (15.2 cm). Collection Chloë Sayer.

PLATE 74a

Central area of a Zapotec woman's huipil, *or tunic. Made from velvet in Tehuantepec, Oaxaca, it is adorned with large satin-stitched flowers worked in silk. This style of decoration may have been inspired long ago by shawls imported from Manila and China. Height of area shown: 14" (35.5 cm). Collection Chloë Sayer.*

PLATE 74b

Central area of a Zapotec woman's huipil, *or tunic, of black sateen from Tehuantepec, Oaxaca. Machine-embroidered in chain stitch with commercial cotton thread, it displays interlocking geometric patterning. Height of area shown: 14" (35.5 cm). Collection Chloë Sayer.*

a

b

PLATE 75

Mixe **rebozo**, *or rectangular shawl, from Oaxaca. Woven on a backstrap loom with commercial cotton thread, it is patterned with warp stripes. Approximate width of area shown: 13" (33 cm). Collection Chloë Sayer.*

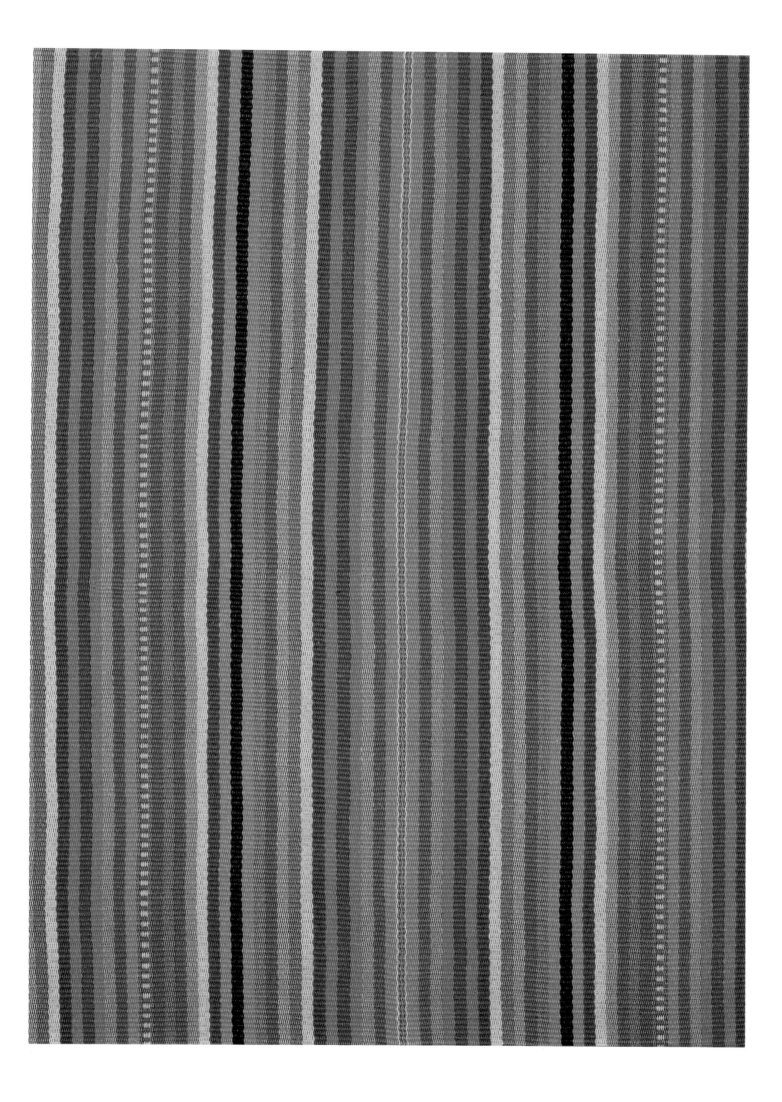

PLATES 76a, 76b

Mixtec servilletas *of hand-spun white cotton from San Juan Colorado, Oaxaca. Woven on a backstrap loom, they feature a range of brocaded motifs worked with commercial cotton thread. Widths: (a) 16" (40.6 cm), (b) 10¾" (27.3 cm). Collection Chloë Sayer.*

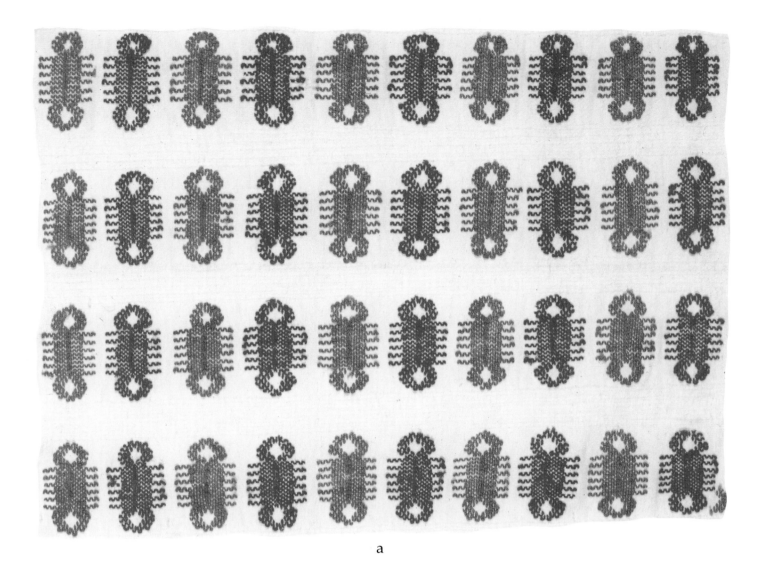

a

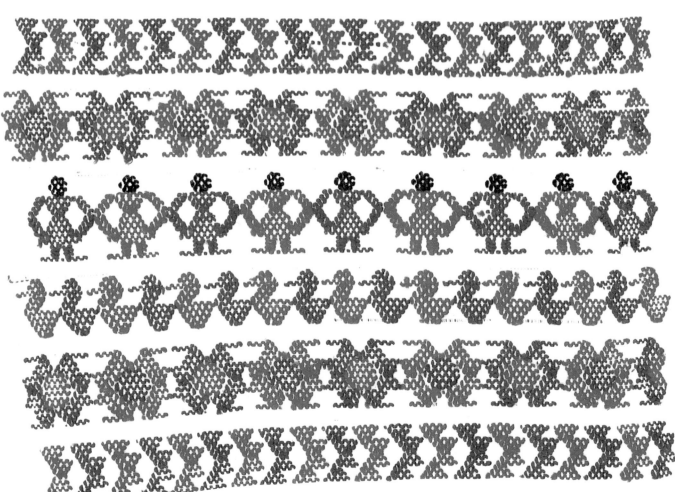

b

PLATE 77

Mixtec servilleta *of hand-spun white cotton from San Juan Colorado, Oaxaca. Woven on a backstrap loom, it is patterned with human figures; these are brocaded with commercial cotton thread. Width of area shown: 17" (43.2 cm). Collection Chloë Sayer.*

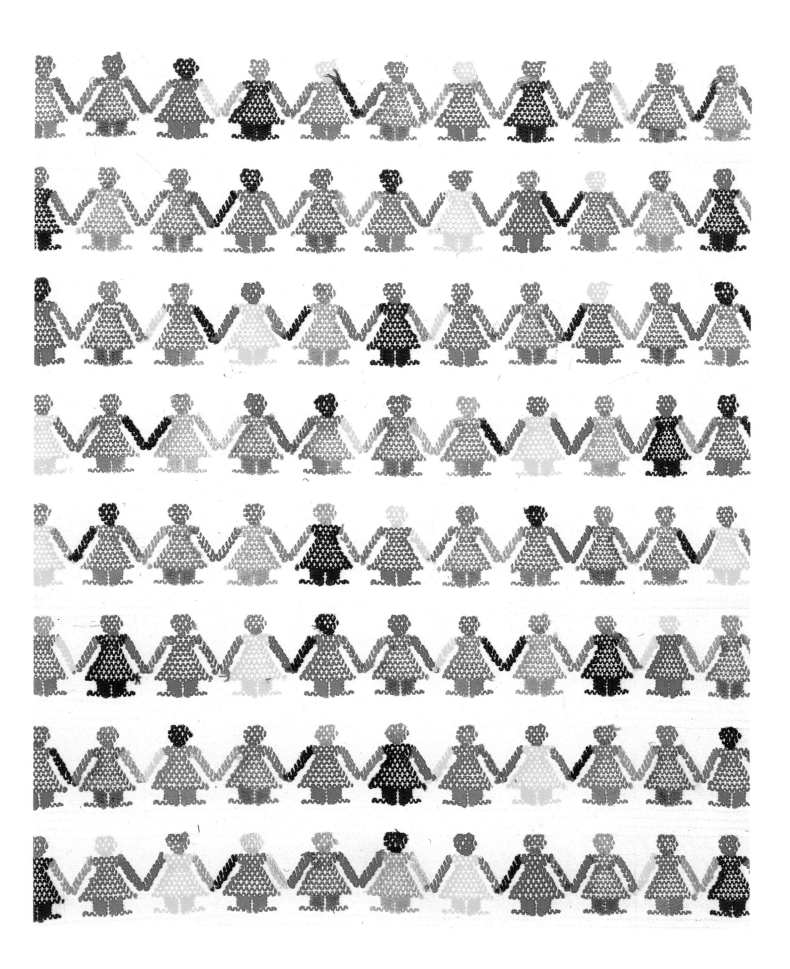

PLATES 78a, 78b, 78c

In most Indian communities male clothing is plainer and less adorned than that of women. The Tacuate, who belong to the Mixtec family, still favour richly decorated garments, however. Shown here are a shirt (a) and trouser bottoms (b) and (c) from Santa María Zacatepec, Oaxaca. Plain-woven from hand-spun cotton on a backstrap loom, they feature rows of minuscule animal, insect and bird motifs. Stylized and multicoloured, they are embroidered in satin, back, cross, herringbone and chain stitch. The central band is differently worked for each trouser. Height of area (a): 19" (48.2 cm). Museum of Mankind, London. Height of area (b) and (c): 4" (10.2 cm). Collection Chloë Sayer.

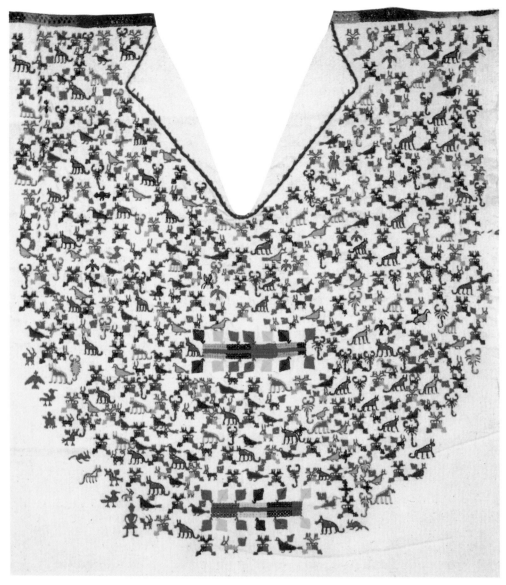

a

b

c

PLATE 79

Section from a woman's wrap-around skirt. Woven on a backstrap loom in the Mixtec community of Pinotepa de Don Luis, Oaxaca, it displays handsome warp stripes. These incorporate hiladillo, *or cochineal-dyed silk, dark-blue cotton dyed with indigo, and lilac cotton dyed with the secretion of shellfish. Height of area shown: 25" (63.5 cm). Museum of Mankind, London.*

PLATE 80

Three-web gala huipil, *or woman's tunic, from the Mixtec village of San Pedro Jicayán, Oaxaca. Woven on the backstrap loom, it incorporates* hiladillo, *or cochineal-dyed silk, white cotton and lilac cotton dyed with the secretion of shellfish. Double-headed birds and serrated X-motifs composed of triangles are brocaded. Such garments are worn for the marriage ceremony or by the wives of dignitaries. Width: 51" (129.5 cm). Museum of Mankind, London.*

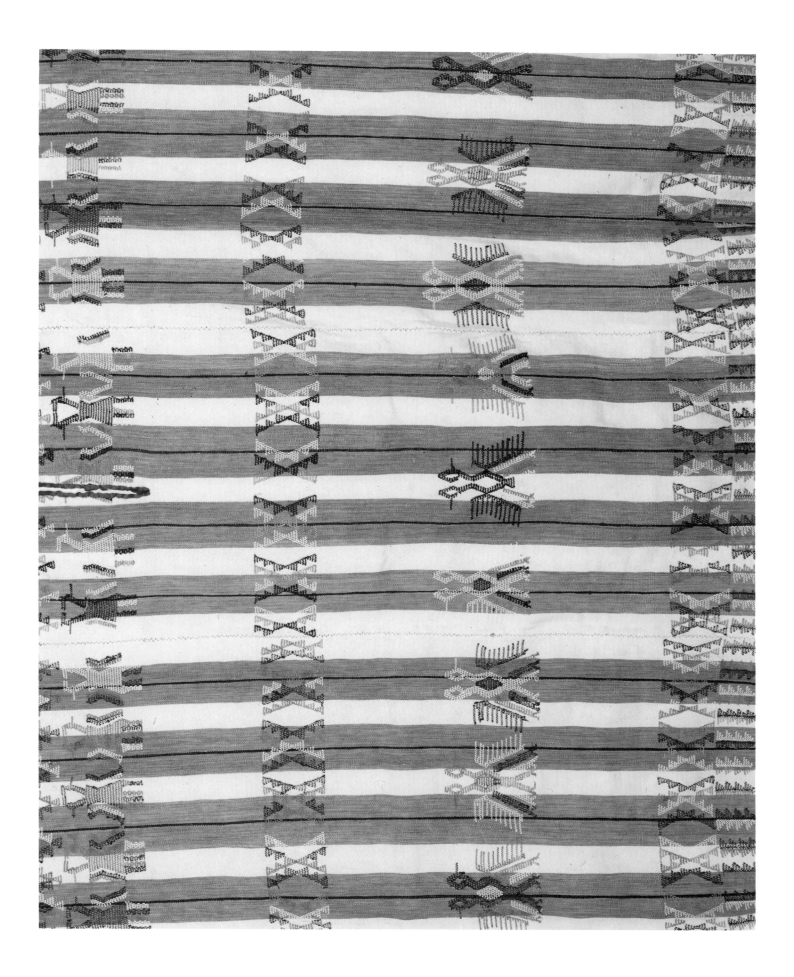

PLATE 81a

Neck area of a woman's huipil, *or tunic, from the Mixtec community of Jamiltepec, Oaxaca. The background cloth was plain-woven on a backstrap loom with hand-spun cotton. Decoration is provided by appliquéd ribbon and by loose stitches done with commercial cotton and synthetic silk threads. Height of area shown: 15½″ (39.4 cm). Collection Chloë Sayer.*

PLATE 81b

Detail from a Mixtec huipil, *or tunic, from San Miguel Metlatonoc, Guerrero. It was woven on a backstrap loom with hand-spun cotton. Brocaded design elements incorporate horses and eight-petal flowers or stars, worked with commercial cotton thread. Width of area shown: 12″ (30.5 cm). Collection Chloë Sayer.*

a

b

PLATE 82

Mixtec woman's huipil, *or tunic, from San Miguel Metlatonoc, Guerrero. Woven in three webs on a backstrap loom from hand-spun cotton, it has been well worn. Designs, brocaded with commercial cotton thread on a plain-woven ground, include rearing horses with plumed tails, birds with outstretched wings, and double-headed eagles. Webs are joined with decorative stitching. 30" × 37½" (76.2 × 95.3 cm). Museum of Mankind, London.*

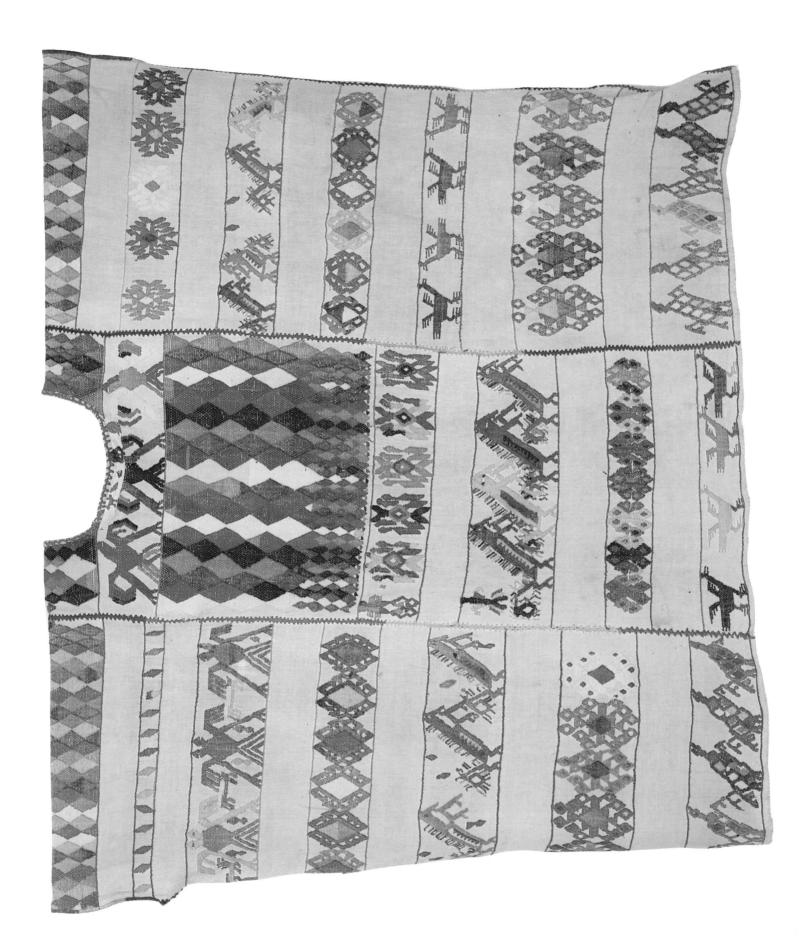

PLATE 83

Amuzgo huipil, *or woman's tunic, from Xochistlahuaca, Guerrero. Plain-woven in three webs on a backstrap loom from hand-spun cotton, it displays a wealth of brocaded patterning worked with commercial cotton thread. Designs include vine, flower and fern motifs. Various elements suggest highly stylized double-headed eagles. Webs are joined with decorative stitching. 36" × 44" (91.4 × 111.7 cm). Collection Chloë Sayer.*

PLATE 84

Central web of an Amuzgo huipil, *or woman's tunic, from Xochistlahuaca, Guerrero. Plain-woven from hand-spun cotton on a backstrap loom, it features brocaded designs worked with commercial cotton thread. Stylized plant designs include eight-petal flowers, vines and ferns. Width of area shown: 14" (35.6 cm). Collection Chloë Sayer.*

PLATE 85a

Partial view of a gala cotton huipil, *or tunic, from the Chinantec village of San Lucas Ojitlán, Oaxaca. Cloth webs, woven and patterned on the backstrap loom, are joined with vertical bands of decorative stitching. Additional decoration is achieved with cross stitch and pattern running stitch; sections of ribbon have been appliquéd. Approximate height of area shown: 30" (76.2 cm). Collection Chloë Sayer.*

PLATE 85b

Detail from a Chinantec woman's head-cloth from Oaxaca. Plain-woven in two webs on a backstrap loom from commercial cotton thread, it displays colourful warp stripes. Museum of Mankind, London.

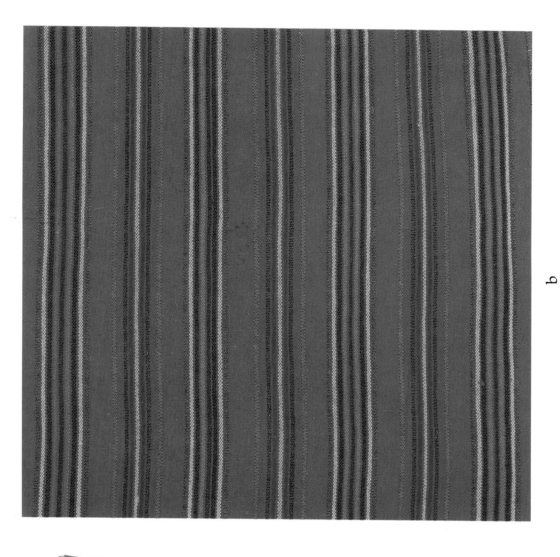

a

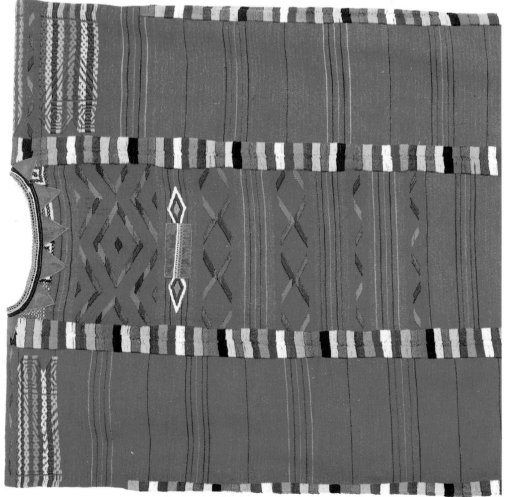

b

PLATE 86

Everyday cotton huipil, *or tunic, from the Chinantec village of San Lucas
Ojitlán, Oaxaca. Plain- and gauze-woven on a backstrap loom, it is
embellished with designs embroidered with commercial thread in pattern
running stitch. Double-headed birds are a recurrent motif in Mexican
textiles. Cloth webs are joined with vertical bands of decorative stitching.
Sections of appliquéd ribbon provide further decoration. 35½" × 31" (90.2 ×
78.7 cm). Museum of Mankind, London.*

PLATE 87a

Detail from a Chinantec woman's huipil, *or tunic, from Rancho Choapan, Oaxaca. The background cloth was plain- and gauze-woven from handspun cotton on a backstrap loom. Geometric and spiral designs are embroidered with commercial cotton thread in pattern running stitch. Vertical bands of satin stitching, seen at the sides, conceal cloth joins. Width of area shown: 10¾" (27.3 cm). Collection Chloë Sayer.*

PLATE 87b

Detail from a Chinantec huipil, *or woman's tunic. Woven on a backstrap loom in San Felipe Usila, Oaxaca, it was constructed with plain, gauze and brocade techniques. Designs include a centrally placed double-headed bird. Finished cloth has been partially over-painted with a purple dye called* fuchina. *Appliquéd ribbon and braid conceal the web joins. Width of area shown: 13" (33 cm). Collection Chloë Sayer.*

b

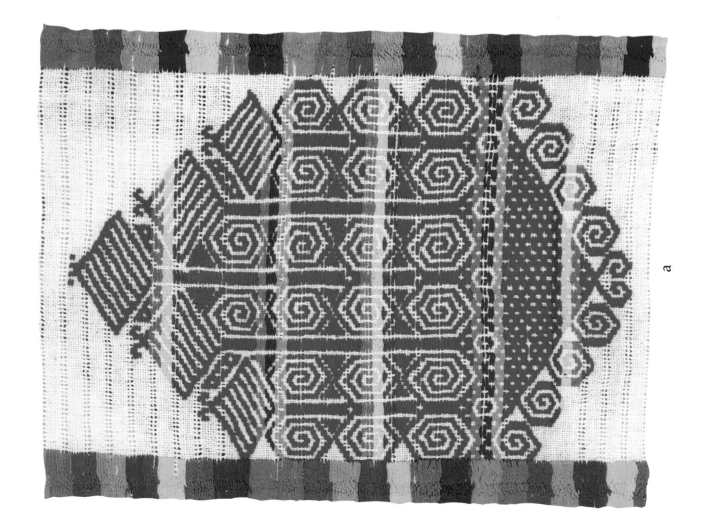

a

PLATE 88

Mazatec cotton huipil *from San Bartolomé Ayautla, Oaxaca, c. 1913. Birds, rabbits, and trees replete with foliage have been embroidered with pattern darning stitch and outline stitch. The background cloth, plain and gauze-woven on a backstrap loom, contributes to the over-all patterning. 31½" × 35" (80 × 90 cm). Museum of Mankind, London.*

PLATE 89

Mazatec huipil, *or tunic, from San Bartolomé Ayautla, Oaxaca, embellished with bird and flower designs. Commercial cotton cloth is embroidered in darning stitch and outline stitch with commercial cotton thread. Height of area shown: 28" (71.1 cm). Collection Hilary Dunlop.*

PLATE 90

Flowers and birds adorn this Mazatec woman's huipil, *or tunic, from San Bartolomé Ayautla, Oaxaca. The commercial cloth ground is worked in surface satin stitch with commercial cotton thread. The designs are formed not just by the embroidery but also by the white cloth itself. Height of area shown: 33" (83.8 cm). Collection Chloë Sayer.*

PLATE 91a

Huave servilleta *of commercial cotton from Santa Maria del Mar, Oaxaca. Plain-woven on a backstrap loom, it displays a profusion of brocaded motifs. Dogs, deer and small baskets are combined with aquatic birds from nearby salt-water lagoons. 28" (71.1 cm) square. Collection Chloë Sayer.*

PLATE 91b

Mazatec waist-sash patterned with hooked geometric designs, c. 1913. Woven on a backstrap loom in San Bartolomé Ayautla, Oaxaca, it features areas of drawn threadwork, reinforced with stitching to form zig-zag lines and triangle-based motifs. Width: 8" (20.3 cm). Museum of Mankind, London.

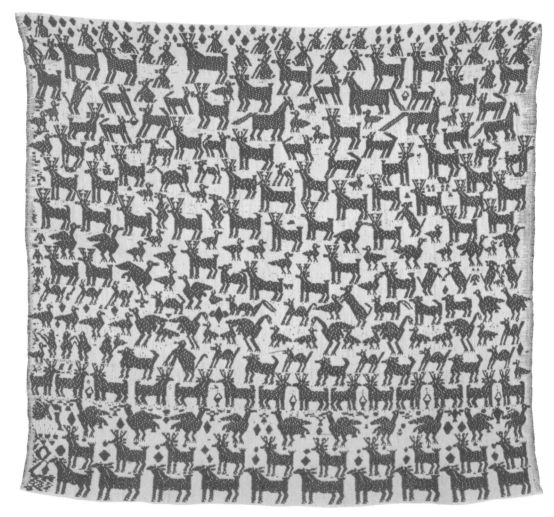

a

b

PLATE 92

Trique huipil, *or woman's tunic, from San Andrés Chicahuaxtla, Oaxaca. Woven in three webs on a backstrap loom, it combines cotton, wool and acrylic yarn. Plain, gauze and brocading techniques have been used. As in many other communities, design elements have local names which often convey little to outsiders. 45" × 38" (114.3 × 96.5 cm). Museum of Mankind, London.*

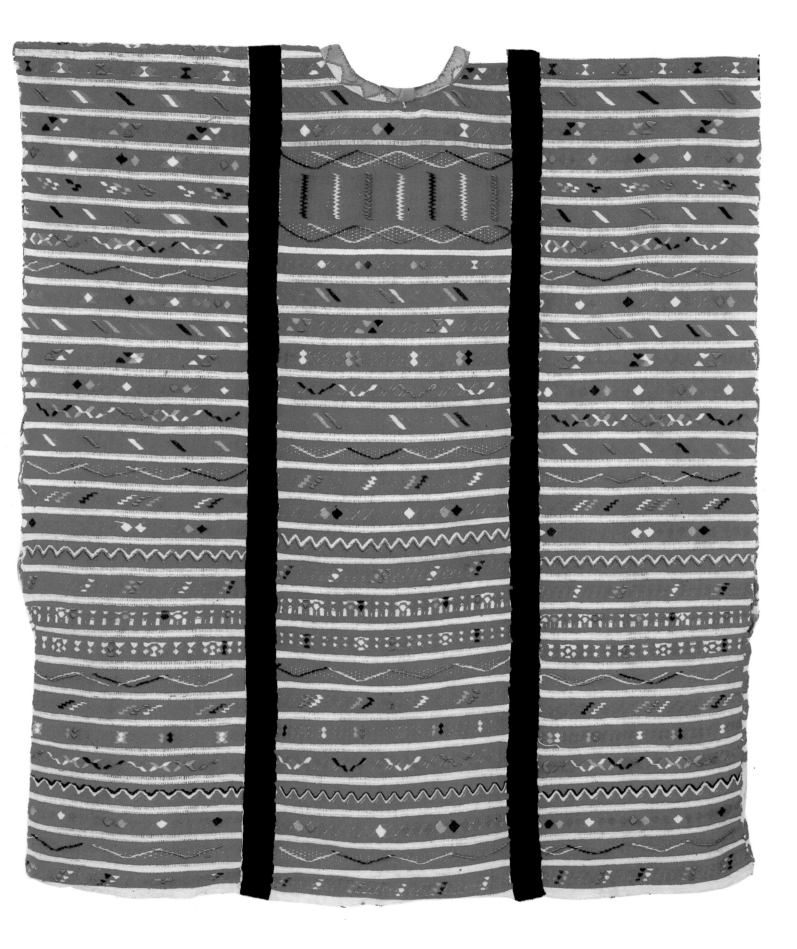

PLATE 93

Tzotzil woman's wrap-around skirt from Venustiano Carranza, plain-woven from indigo-dyed cotton. Bands of over-and-over stitching, worked with acrylic thread, combine with wave patterning, fernlike motifs, birds and flower forms in outline and satin stitch to cover ever-increasing areas. Fine textiles are still part of daily life in Chiapas. The Tzotzil, who belong to the Maya family, are skilled weavers and embroiderers. 45¼" × 42½" (115 × 108 cm). Museum of Mankind, London.

PLATE 94

Bag from the Tzeltal community of Tenejapa in the highlands of Chiapas. Plain-woven on a backstrap loom from cotton and acrylic yarn, it is embellished with areas of confite, *or looped weft patterning. With this technique, supplementary weft threads are looped to form raised super-structural designs. 17" × 14" (43.2 × 35.6 cm). Collection Chloë Sayer.*

PLATE 95a

End section of a man's ceremonial sash from the Tzeltal community of Tenejapa in the highlands of Chiapas. Woven on a backstrap loom from cotton and wool, it features weft bands and brocaded motifs. Width: 13" (33.1 cm). Collection Chloë Sayer.

PLATE 95b

Brocade-patterned cloth, woven on the backstrap loom in the Tzotzil community of San Andrés Larrainzar, Chiapas. 14" × 8" (35.5 × 20.3 cm). Collection Chloë Sayer.

a

b

PLATE 96

Two-web cotton huipil, *or woman's tunic, from the Tzotzil community of Santa Catarina Pantelhó, Chiapas. Woven on the backstrap loom, it features warp stripes. Brocaded designs in the top and third rows represent toads; those in the second and fourth rows are termed* yok bolom *(jaguar's pawprint). 24" × 26" (61 × 66 cm). Collection Chloë Sayer.*

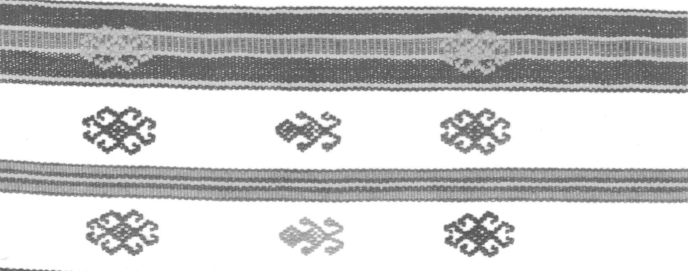
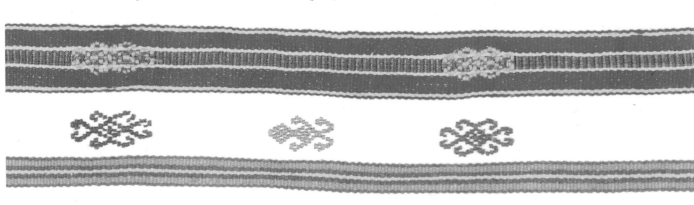
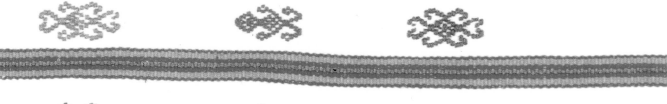

PLATE 97

*Man's waist-sash from the Tzotzil community of Magdalenas, Chiapas.
Woven from cotton on the backstrap loom, it features brocaded designs
worked with wool. According to Walter F. Morris, the two horizontal bands
with spiral patterning are termed* joch'bil *(worm-eaten); the row of figures
along the top are* santoetik *(saints). Area shown: 5½" × 7" (14 × 17.8 cm).
Collection Chloë Sayer.*

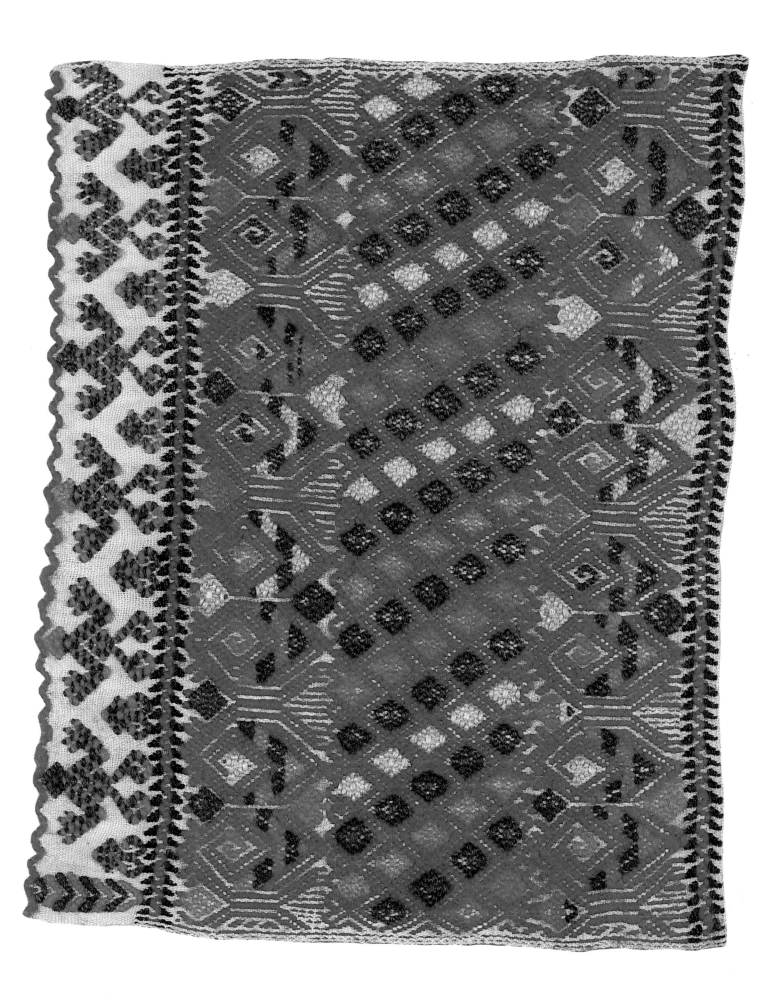

PLATE 98a

Detail from a woman's huipil, *or tunic, from the Tzotzil community of Magdalenas. Interlocking diamond-and-hook motifs are brocade-woven with naturally dyed wool yarns. This element is termed* muk'ta luch *(the grand design). Height of area shown: 7½" (19 cm). Collection Chloë Sayer.*

PLATE 98b

Man's waist-sash from the Tzotzil community of Magdalenas, Chiapas. Woven from cotton on the backstrap loom, it features brocaded designs worked with naturally dyed wool yarns. Width: 10" (25.5 cm). Collection Chloë Sayer.

a

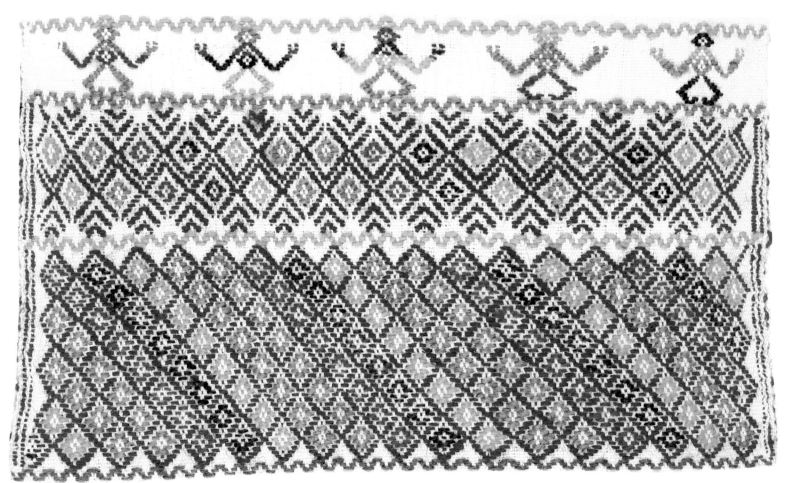

b

PLATE 99

Brocade-patterned section of a woman's huipil, *or tunic, woven from cotton on the backstrap loom in the Tzotzil community of San Andrés Larrainzar, Chiapas. Patterning is provided by interlocking diamond-and-hook motifs; termed* p'ejel luch *(square design), they can be identified more clearly in Plate 100; similar designs from Magdalenas are shown in Plate 98a. Height of area shown: 9" (22.9 cm). Collection Chloë Sayer.*

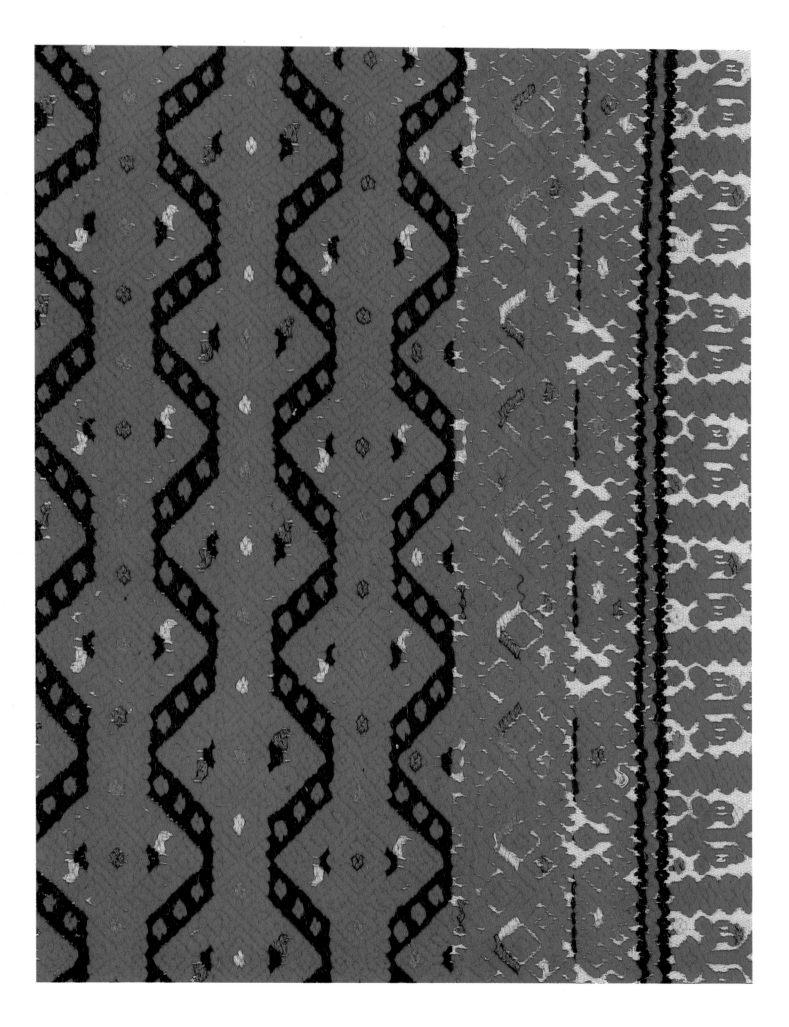

PLATE 100

Brocade-patterned section of cloth, woven from cotton on the backstrap loom in the Tzotzil community of San Andrés Larrainzar, Chiapas. Interlocking diamond-and-hook motifs are combined with other forms of geometric patterning. Area shown: 17" × 13" (43.2 × 33 cm). Collection Nicole England.

Short Bibliography

Information about Mexican Indian costume and design motifs is provided by the following:

ANAWALT, Patricia Rieff, *Indian Clothing Before Cortés: Mesoamerican Costumes from the Codices.* University of Oklahoma Press. Norman, 1981.

CORDRY, Donald B. and Dorothy M., *Mexican Indian Costumes.* University of Texas Press. Austin, 1968.

COVARRUBIAS, Miguel, *Mexico South: The Isthmus of Tehuantepec.* Alfred A. Knopf. New York, 1946.

ENCISO, Jorge, *Design Motifs of Ancient Mexico.* Dover Publications Inc. New York, 1953.

—— *Designs from Pre-Columbian Mexico.* Dover Publications Inc. New York, 1971.

FIELD, Frederick, *Pre-Hispanic Mexican Stamp Designs.* Dover Publications Inc. New York, 1974.

JETER, James, and JUELKE, Paula Marie, *The Saltillo Sarape* (exhibition catalogue). Museum of Art, Santa Barbara, 1978.

JOHNSON, Irmgard Weitlaner, *Design Motifs on Mexican Indian Textiles* (2 vols.). Akademische Druck and Verlagsanstalt. Graz, 1976.

—— and FRANCO, José Luis, 'Un huipil precolombino de Chilapa, Guerrero'. *Revista Mexicana de Estudios Antropológicos* II: 279–91. Mexico City, 1967.

MAPELLI MOZZI, Carlota, and CASTELLÓ YTURBIDE, Teresa, *El traje indígena en México* (2 vols.). Instituto Nacional de Antropología e Historia. Mexico City, 1965–8.

LECHUGA, Ruth D., *El traje indígena de México: su evolución desde la época prehispánica hasta la actualidad.* Panorama Editorial S.A. Mexico City, 1982.

LUMHOLTZ, Carl, 'Symbolism of the Huichol Indians'. *Memoirs of the American Museum of Natural History* 3, Anthropology 2 (1): 1–228. New York, 1900.

—— *Unknown Mexico* (2 vols.). Macmillan and Co. London, 1903.

—— 'Decorative Art of the Huichol Indians.' *Memoirs of the American Museum of Natural History* 3. Anthropology 2 (3): 279–327. New York, 1904.

MORRIS, Walter F., junr., *A Millennium of Weaving in Chiapas.* Private printing by the author for distribution by Sna Jolobil, the Chiapas Maya Weavers' Association. Mexico, 1984.

—— *Luchetik: El lenguaje textil de los Altos de Chiapas (The Woven Word from Highland Chiapas).* Private printing by the author for distribution by Sna Jolobil, the Chiapas Maya Weavers' Association. Mexico, 1984.

—— *Living Maya.* Harry N. Abrahams Inc. New York, 1987.

SAYER, Chloë, *Mexican Costume.* British Museum Publications. London, 1985.

TUROK, Martha, 'Diseño y simbolo en el huipil ceremonial de Magdalenas, Chiapas', *Boletín* 3. Departamento de Investigación de las Tradiciones Populares. Dirección General de Arte Popular, SEP. Mexico City, 1974.